This book has an intrinsically
the reader, craving a contin
end. It implants in the reade
understanding of the power of the tongue. I have been personally blessed by this powerfully irresistible and compelling teaching.

—Professor Philip Alalibo
Dept. of Humanities & Social Sciences
Centennial College of Applied Arts & Technology

I have known Marva for over 20 years and seen the power of the blessing at work in and through her life. This teaching will transform your life, family, ministry, business and career. Some books teach great theory, but this book is about what Marva knows, and lives out. This book goes deep into the Word of God and expounds on the right we have been given by the new birth experience in Jesus to 'bless and not curse.'

Marva's book is relevant, informative and practical, and will have an impact on the nations of the world. It is a message that speaks to all ages: from the child in the womb, through every stage of life, up to the elder who is full of life experiences.

Words have power. The Word of God is the ultimate source of creativity and power, and in this book Marva will inspire you to take up your inherent right to bless the world around you.

—Thomas Aro
Senior Pastor, Glad Tidings Tabernacle

The need to restore access to the spoken family blessing that God has always intended for you is crucial now more than ever before. As with any investment that compounds over time, wealth untapped also becomes increasing poverty. *Recover Your Blessing Birthright* is such a timely and incredible book to help you skillfully tap into the compounded wealth of God for your life. My great friend, Rev. Marva Militia Tyndale, carries a genuine restoration anointing. This is seen through her writings that will cause you to not only see, but experience longed for healing and transformation as you tap into your intended birthright blessing! It is Possible!

—Andrea Boweya
Registered Psychotherapist
Author— *Legacy Moments* and *The Heart of a Good Thing*

Every family needs this teaching. God has used Marva to revive the sacred tradition of the family blessing and this critical element is so needed to realign us with God's plan for the family. I had the pleasure of walking through this teaching with Marva and was overwhelmed at the impact that it had on my life. Immediately, I began to think about the transformational power of spoken blessings and the need for me to proactively walk this journey with my family. Now, we have a resource to assist us in doing this with knowledge and confidence. As families walk this journey, generational curses will be broken, and our children will be able to more fully embrace their identity, calling, and purpose in Jesus Christ.

—Racquel Brown
Christian Parenting Speaker, Empowerandequip.ca

I have the privilege of knowing Pastor Marva, listening to her speak, watching as she ministers, and she truly exemplifies what she writes. As I read this book, I heard her heart, her passion, her voice, and I know you will also.

—Pastor Dave Connolly
Islington Evangel Centre

Rev. Marva Tyndale's book, *Recover Your Blessing Birthright,* introduces an incredible life-changing gift for sowing God's love in people's hearts and into their future. With criticism and cursing words prevalent in our culture, this book offers a godly alternative—blessing others with the gift of our words. She encourages her readers to recover God's design of speaking words that release life, from conception and beyond. Taken seriously, this model will transform both our lives and culture.

—Rev. Wendell Gibbs, M.Div.
First Baptist Church, Toronto

Marva's experiences and the strategic guidelines she presents in this book will help everyone, from the individual to the Church, and our society as a whole. From beginning to end, the book is readable and understandable. It has a gentle explosive power that will bring change, eternal change, to this generation and beyond. This book certainly has the potential to transform an entire population and culture. The book's subtitle is doable—transformation of our lives, our families and our culture with the gift of our words.

—Pastor Ralph Glagau
Humberlea Worship Centre

Marva Militia Tyndale plunges deep into the heart of God, and extracts the true and accurate meaning of receiving and giving intentional blessings. With carefully chosen life-transforming words and contagious passion, she creates hunger and thirst in our hearts to give and receive blessings. Marva searches biblical history and highlights experiences and observations of contemporary writers, as well as her own, to challenge us not to neglect our invaluable birthright. As a motivational instructor, Marva directs us to the Word of God and convinces us that we are Blessing Ambassadors; that indeed we 'possess a tongue through which blessings and healings will come.' Every home, business, and community should make this resource available to help create a culture of enhancing interpersonal relationships. MEN!!! Here we have a unique opportunity to take up the mantle of leadership and learn how to impart verbal blessings over our children, grandchildren, wives, relatives, communities, our nation, and other nations of the world.

—Dr. Dudley Mayers
Kingdom Bible Training Center
Global Chaplaincy Center

"It is possible!" These words express our sentiments in endorsing this book. Marva has captured the essence of the right of every human being to be blessed and to bless others. Her own personal journey has given her the authority to write this resource that will help everyone to make spoken blessings a part of their lifestyle. May spoken blessings become a way of life for every family.

—Revs. Anthony and Cheryl Nelson
Founders of Faith Five Fellowship of Ministries Inc.
Pastors of Faith Five Restoration Centre
Faith5centre.net

My friend, Marva Tyndale, has presented a masterful treatment of the significance and enormous value of the spoken blessing. I encourage every husband, wife and leader to learn these practical and relevant truths. They will transform your life, as well as the lives of those closest to you. You will certainly be blessed!

—Pastor Randy Neilson
Bramalea Christian Fellowship
Brampton, Canada

Rev. Marva Tyndale has written a must-read book for anyone who has not yet received the blessing that God intended as their birthright. God is neither cheap nor miserly. The world cannot equal His blessing and its ability to endow power for prosperity and success. Jesus won the victory at the Cross! The curse was transformed into blessing, and He now leads us into a triumphant process to possess it all. Marva's book serves as a guide and motivation to pursue a course of life empowered by the blessing.

—Rev. Corville E. Peters
Producer/Host, AT THE CROSS Live
Author— *What Does the Cross Mean to You*

The chapter on "Worth Its Weight in Gold," captures the Jewish mandate which is really the mandate of every believer in Yeshua. That is, we are called to be like God and bring "blessings" to our family and the people around us. It starts with hearing and speaking words of blessing over our children and to the community on a regular basis. The spiritual reality of the spoken blessing needs to sink into our spirits, so that it can be manifested outwardly. It is only when we realize that we are called to be a blessing (it is in our spiritual DNA), that we can be a blessing to others. Speaking blessing is part of our testimony that we are indeed God's children.

—Rev. Freddie Sanvictores
Co-Founder, Congregation Yeshua
Author— *Believers in Yeshua's Jewish Calling: A Journey in Rediscovering Our Jewish Roots and Our Forgotten Mission of "To the Jews First."*

You are blessed
to be a blessing!
Gen 22:17

Recover Your Blessing Birthright

Also by Marva Tyndale

Books

Keeping Our Hope Alive:
Strategies to Restore Teens and Young Adults

911 HOPE: When Your Youth or Young Adult is in Trouble

Audio Book

911 HOPE: When Your Youth or Young Adult is in Trouble

Study Guides

Breaking Negative Family Patterns
(Series 1 - 3)

Destroying the Tap Root of Occult Covenants
Uprooting Sexual Iniquity
Returning to the Fatherhood of God

Compact Disc

Prayer Therapy for Brain-Mind-Heart Renewal
(CD & Booklet)

For more information on these resources or to place an order:

Real Identity Discovery Ministries
Box 29622—377 Burnhamthorpe Road East
Mississauga, ON. L5A 4H2 Canada
info@realidteaching.org
416.277.6891
www.realidteaching.org

Recover Your Blessing Birthright

Transforming Lives and Culture with the Gift of Words

Marva Militia Tyndale

Summerhill Publishing

ISBN: 978-0-9953000-2-6
E-book ISBN: 978-0-9953000-3-3
(E-book available from the Kindle Store, KOBO and the iBooks Store)

To order additional copies:
info@realidteaching.org • 416-277-6891 • www.realidteaching.org

Published by: Summerhill Publishing, Ontario, Canada
Printed in Canada

Dedication

With great joy, I dedicate this book to:

My Abba Father, the Source from whom all blessings come. To Jesus Christ, my Triumphant Redeemer, because of whom and in whom I am blessed with every spiritual blessing. To the Blessed Holy Spirit who enabled me to traverse time and space in my spirit and recover my blessing birthright.

Gwendolyn Houston, who almost twenty years ago discerned God's call on my life and said that her assignment was to "get me to the palace" —to do for me what Jonathan had done for David. It was her gift of *The Power of Blessing* book in 2004 that introduced me to the spoken blessing, helped me to recover my missed blessings and launched me onto the path of a blessing ambassador. Every word of blessing I have ever spoken or written is part of her legacy. Thank you, Gwendolyn, for making this book possible. May you enjoy the rich harvest of your labor of love, here and in eternity.

My children, grandchildren, and generations to come, who by God's grace will inherit a legacy of blessings and prayers to fulfill their God-given destiny and purpose.

My spiritual sons and daughters in whose lives and families God is reproducing much fruit for His glory.

The men and women in each generation whose diligence in exercising their responsibility as blessing ambassadors will be instrumental in restoring spoken blessings as a way of life for generations to come.

Contents

Part 1: Discovery

Part 2: Recovery

Acknowledgments

In building this resource tool, it was my privilege to stand on the shoulders of several forerunners who have been releasing wisdom and healing around the world through the instrument of spoken blessings. My heartfelt gratitude goes out to these leaders.

My personal discovery, experience, and understanding of the power of blessing began with Terry and Melissa Bone of I.D. Ministries. It was later enhanced through the teachings of Arthur Burk of the Sapphire Leadership Group. I am honored to have their permission to draw wisdom, principles and language from the treasures God has given them. Although you will have the opportunity to meet them indirectly through this book, I encourage you to visit Terry and Melissa Bone at www.powerofblessing.com and Arthur Burk at www.theslg.com to tap directly into the wealth of resources they have available.

I would also like to thank Colleen Miller-Blake whose invitation to speak at her 2017 Women of Worth Conference was the tipping point in the birth of the Blessing Recovery Clinic and eventually this book. Colleen, I appreciate your sensitivity to the Holy Spirit that enabled you to be a divine catalyst.

My commission for this book was clear. Yet, no one is an island. So, without the valuable support and assistance of many individuals, I may not have satisfied the desire of my heavenly Father for this book.

Thank you …

. . . to the various individuals whose suggestions and editorial contributions strengthened the manuscript: Philip Alalibo, Terry and Melissa Bone, Andrea Boweya, Gwendolyn Houston, Anthony and Cheryl Nelson, Nadia Petri, Freddie Sanvictores, Korrie Silver, Maurice Tyndale, and Rosie Watson.

. . . to the pastors and leaders who invested valuable time in reading the manuscript and sharing their views.

. . . to each person whose testimonial of personal encounters with the power of spoken blessings enriched the book in a very special way.

. . . to the Board of Directors of Real Identity Discovery Ministries (RIDM), who have faithfully steered the ministry and assisted me in fulfilling God's call on my life.

. . . to the RIDM partners and friends who have stood with me over the years. May the Lord greatly reward you for your generous and faithful support.

. . . to all the faithful intercessors who have prayed countless prayers for me, my family and the ministry. Your prayers have been like wind for my sail.

. . . to Andrew and Juli-Anne James whose lives and children so gracefully reflect the fruit of spoken blessings. Thank you for the Summerhill Publishing stamp of excellence on this book.

. . . to Sonny Martin of Attitude Communications for consistent exceptional service.

Last, but not the least, I would like to express my deepest gratitude to Maurice, my dear husband and spiritual covering. Thank you for encouraging me to "go for it" whenever the Lord commissions me to an assignment. Also, for providing much-needed practical support along the way. I bless you as we journey on together to a strong finish in Christ!

Foreword

I had served in pastoral ministry for over a decade before I came to realize the meaning of "Family Blessing." It uncovered a surprising new level of spiritual authority for me as a husband, parent and pastor. It brought transformation to lives quicker than anything I had previously seen. One day, the Lord instructed my wife, Melissa, and I, to resign our roles as Pastors and take this vital message to the world.

Not long afterwards, we met Marva. We were astounded at her wholehearted approach to learning and applying the truths we taught. Marva's testimony since then has been a living proof of the power of Family Blessing to bring transformation.

Marva's call from God is evidenced by her dogged determination to ensure that everyone within the sound of her voice and the reach of her pen hears this message. When this determination is combined with a sharp mind and excellent communication skills, the inevitable result is this book.

This book carries what I call a 'Nehemiah anointing' —a bold faith and willingness to look at the broken-down walls around the dwelling place of God's people and say, "This stops in my generation!"

I bless this book that it may become a cornerstone in the rebuilding of the walls of many broken family systems, so that future generations may live productive, fruitful and peaceful lives, protected from the enemy of our souls.

— Rev. Terry R. Bone
Author, Missionary, Life Coach
www.powerofblessing.com

[birthright]

noun

birth·right \ ˈbərth-ˌrīt \

:a right, privilege, or possession to which a person is entitled by birth.

:a right of all people.

www.merriam-webster.com

www.learnersdictionary.com/definition/birthright

Preface

Did you know that you have a spiritual birthright you may not have received? It is a birthright of verbal blessings (also known as Family Blessing), and it holds the key to having a fulfilling journey through life. It is yours just because you were born, and there is nothing you have to do to earn it.

You may be thinking, "Why haven't I received this birthright if it is really that simple?" Unfortunately, the spoken blessing was not commonplace in the family culture into which most of us were born or raised. Many of us have missed out.

What if there was a way to recover those missed blessings as well as help others to do the same? What if those blessings could become a normal way of life and be woven into our cultural fabric?

This book was written for exactly these reasons, and it follows in the line of several other books that have been written about spoken blessings. So, why another book on the subject?

Recover Your Blessing Birthright: Transforming Lives and Culture with the Gift of Words was commissioned by the Holy Spirit with a single word: **accentuate.**

My Assignment: To create a tool to restore the culture of spoken blessings that God established in the beginning, and to intensify its prominence.

My Goals: To increase awareness of the power of spoken blessings to shape lives and destiny, increase access to the blessing, and impart the mantle to more individuals as blessing ambassadors. In relation to this goal of mantle impartation, the concept of "mantle" refers to the fundamental responsibility to speak words of blessing that God designed all human beings to carry.

My Vision: To be remedial and preventive.

My Mission: To supplement, not re-invent.

We are in this together. We will use the gift of our words to transform lives and restore a culture of spoken blessing.

Your blessing ambassador,

Marwa Militia Tyndale

Introduction

It is possible!

We need it now! We need answers for broken lives, for broken hearts, for chronic insecurities, for arrested destinies and more. I am convinced that in His love and mercy, God designed the spoken blessing as a timeless antidote for the many maladies He knew would plague fallen humanity. The redemptive power of intentionally spoken words backed by divine authority far surpasses our imagination. Yet, it is ours to reach for relentlessly, starting now!

I am fully persuaded that the regular deposit of spoken blessings into the heart of each person from their conception is one of God's kingdom mysteries. It is the secret for reorienting and realigning humanity and our culture with God's "in the beginning" design—one life at a time.

It is possible!

This resource is my hope seed and faith extender for making that vision a reality. The fulfillment of this vision of hope begins with us—seniors, adults, and young adults alike. How do we get there? I'm glad you asked. It's a process that involves recovering our missed blessings; picking up our mantle; being deployed to youth, children, and those yet to be born; and becoming progressively more equipped to operate in the enlarged spheres of influence that God has for us.

I am fully committed to the journey; will you join me?

God has rightly positioned us in our generation to steward the young generation of yet-to-be-parents and the children they will have. They have been entrusted to us for the cause of restoring God's "in the beginning" design for His people and the earth. This blessing resource is part of God's provision. Among other things, it is a forerunner to the early-stage parenting model (*Parent Start*) that God has commissioned me to build. *Parent Start* anticipates a new generation of moms and dads who will come out of the parenting starting blocks in God's appointed time, equipped and ready to exercise their blessing mantle right from the conception of their child. That's where we're headed. I'm all in and I pray that you are too.

A Passion-driven Resource

Recover Your Blessing Birthright: Transforming Lives and Culture with the Gift of Words offers remedial and preventive solutions. The book has a strong redemptive focus and is guided by a compelling motto: **recover to deploy to multiply and to transform**. The goal is for more individuals to reclaim their birthright—to **recover** their missed blessings and the sense of legitimacy that the blessings convey. Thereafter, be **deployed** as ambassadors who are mantled with the heavenly Father's spiritual authority. Ultimately, their mandate is to **multiply** the seed and the fruit of blessing to bring forth a bountiful harvest of **transformation** to the glory of God.

The concept of birthright is typically associated with firstborn privileges. However, the concept has a broader application in this book. In the context of this book, birthright relates to the privileges we all have as God's offspring, created in His image and likeness, to receive words of blessing and to operate like Him in speaking words of blessing.

An Instrument of Transformation

God is breathing a fresh wind of His Spirit on the spoken blessing as an instrument of transformation in this season. Our part is to begin where we are and restore the blessing as a way of life in our immediate circles of influence. God is faithful to release the flow of His power through the words we speak to transform lives and various aspects of our culture. The deep hunger in the spirit, heart and soul of many in our families, churches, and wider communities will be gloriously satisfied.

For All People Groups and Generations

This resource is for all people groups, including generations to come. However, it is specifically aimed at prospective parents, parents and grandparents, because of the responsibility they have as God's "special agents" to steward the identity and destiny of the children He has entrusted to them.

Men, fathers and prospective fathers, your part in God's design is critical! Your words carry an added weight of authority, and this is true even when your words are not wholesome. Our culture desperately needs to hear your life-giving words, whether you are a biological father or not. Your children and the next generation need your words of blessing, because your voice will accomplish in a moment the good that may otherwise not be realized or may take a very long time to be realized.

Many of us who are presently in our adult and senior years have missed the spoken words of blessing that God designed as our fundamental birthright at pivotal stages of life. The passion of my heart is to ensure that although we missed our blessings, future generations will not. It is my deep conviction that they should not have to go through life with the hunger for legitimization that many of us have struggled so hard to overcome.

One participant in a blessing recovery "clinic" I was running expressed her conviction well: "I am forty-plus and only now receiving what I should have had from the time I was conceived in my mother's womb.

Now let's do better for the next generation."

Speaking blessing to babies in the womb, to infants and to growing children will divinely empower future generations to have greater alignment with God than we (the present generation) ever experienced. I can only imagine what God will accomplish through a generation of children and young people whose spirits are saturated with intentional words of blessing from the time of their conception.

An Extra Special Appeal

Unabashedly, I make a further appeal to the people group into which I was born; the black race. Slavery and colonialism have created horrible breaches in our history, especially in the areas of family and community. Nevertheless, there is hope for healing and transformation. Through this ancient gift of blessing we can bring unprecedented dimensions of healing to families and individuals from the inside out. We may not be able to change our history, but we can recover this lost birthright and use it as a powerful instrument to heal the past and pass on a rich spiritual legacy.

In Isaiah 58:12, The Message Bible gives us this powerful picture of hope:

> *You'll use the old rubble of past lives to build anew, rebuild the foundations from out of your past. You'll be known as those who can fix anything, restore old ruins, rebuild and renovate, make the community livable again.*

The New Living Translation puts it this way: "...You will be known as a rebuilder of walls and a restorer of homes."

Our historical legacy, coupled with the lost culture of blessing, left us "...like a city broken into and left without walls" (Proverbs 25:28 ESV). However, like the rebuilders in the Book of Nehemiah, we can have success by adopting the strategy of repairing the breaches closest to our own home (see Nehemiah 3:28-30).

May we discover, connect with, and build on the generational treasures hidden in each of our families. At a blessing ceremony for an expectant mother, I met someone who was delighted to discover and connect deeply with her rich generational legacy of verbal blessing. She shared with me words that her grandmother and great-grandmother often spoke to her while she was growing up. Although her elders may not have used the word "blessing," verbal blessing was actually a normal way of life for them.

This story reinforced the principle of Isaiah 65:8, that something good is in the "cluster" of our generational history even if we do not readily recognize it: "...New wine is found in the cluster...'Do not destroy it, For a blessing is in it.'"

Let's dig deep for the treasures!

The Redemptive Power of the Tongue

Aaron Früh, a Jewish author, echoes my faith in the redemptive power of spoken blessing:

> *It is my premise that much of the iniquity that is passed from generation to generation is a result of verbal abuse. And if that is the case, if it is through the tongue that we were cursed, then I believe it is through the tongue that blessing and healing will come.*[1]

In moving towards making this deep healing a reality, we can also adopt a hope-inspiring phrase that my dear friend, Andrea Boweya, has coined so precisely for *The Restoration of Fatherhood* initiative: "One moment at a time. One person at a time. It is possible!"

We can

recover

this lost birthright

and use it as a

powerful instrument

to heal the past and pass on a

rich spiritual

legacy.

God said it this way through the angel Gabriel: "For with God nothing will be impossible" (Luke 1:37).

Jesus confirmed: "What appears humanly impossible is more than possible with God. For God can do what man cannot" (Luke 18:27 TPT).

One word at a time. Redemption is possible!

The Blessing Mantle and Authority

As an offspring of Abraham through faith in Jesus, the mantle and authority to bless are your birthright. "All the families on earth will be blessed through you" (Genesis 12:3b NLT). In fact, the blessing was part of God's covenant provision from the beginning as we observed in His blessing of Adam, Noah, and Abraham (see Genesis 1:28; 9:1-2; 12:3). It was His covenant design and intent that men and women in each generation would multiply the blessing by passing it on to others.

The good news is that God has already deposited in your spirit everything you need to be a blessing ambassador. This resource facilitates the multiplication of the blessing by unveiling what you already have within you and formally releasing the mantle to those who would agree to become an ambassador of the blessing (see Appendix One).

Book Overview

This book is a transformational tool designed to facilitate and enhance your personal experience of receiving and giving the gift of spoken blessings. It isn't a book that you just read and put aside. It isn't for casual reading or merely for information. It is a call to action! I know that we live in a fast-moving age with little time to go deep. However, the investment principle applies here. You can choose how much you want to invest in this tool, bearing in mind that you will get out of it what you put into it.

Here is a quick overview:

- There are two parts to the book: **Discovery** and **Recovery**. The book was birthed out of the second part, and you will need all of the first in order to get the maximum benefit out of the second.
- The very important "Blessing Mantle" is in Appendix One.
- There are also several other Appendices with valuable resources.
- The first five chapters of Part One are somewhat of a backstory with snippets of my journey that will help you to understand my passion for the blessing.
- Chapter Five introduces the principle of blessing spirit-to-spirit and other revelations that may be relatively new, so read with an open mind.
- Chapter Six provides a powerful transition that explores the legacy of blessing in Jewish culture.
- Chapters Seven to Ten have the "nuts and bolts" for your training as a blessing ambassador.
- Chapter Eleven is an absolute prerequisite for Part Two.
- In Part Two, you have the opportunity to participate in a spiritual recovery "clinic" and catch up on blessings you may have missed from the time of your conception to the present. A chapter is dedicated to each of the seven major life stages.
- In Part Two, you get to recover the missing "something" that you may have been waiting for all your life. One person described the experience of going through the "clinic" as a journey. However, it isn't a journey that you can dash through. Take your time and trust your spirit to lead you into *Selah*[2] breaks as needed.

Curious about the "clinic?" Go ahead and take a sneak preview, but remember that Chapter Eleven in Part One is a prerequisite for the "clinic."

Also, don't miss the powerful testimonials at the end of the book.

Happy reading and may you have a fulfilling journey of discovery and recovery.

Part 1

DISCOVERY

Seek, and you'll discover…
Every persistent seeker will discover what he longs for.
Matthew 7:7–8 TPT

Chapter 1

A Hungry Multitude

"No one knows how long I waited for this!" These words could have been spoken by me or any of the hundreds of people who had waited all their life to hear words of blessing that legitimized their existence. I mean, words that anchored them in love, and clothed them with a sense of significance, value and dignity. The young lady who spoke these words was the voice of many, saying for them what they could only have said with tears after recovering their missed blessings.

The inspiration for this resource came from a picture I saw through the "eyes of my spirit." It was a picture of many spiritually famished men, women and children of all ages. Most did not have the words to describe their longing. They only sensed the deep gnawing ache of a missing "something." A few had the insight that they longed to hear words of blessing that would somehow bring their life together, yet they felt disqualified. There were others present with this hungry multitude. They interacted with them, acknowledged their hunger, but had nothing to offer. They sent them away and my heart was broken by their helplessness.

As I looked at the picture, I heard snippets of the familiar conversation between Jesus and His disciples at the feeding of the five thousand in the Gospel of Matthew:

"Send them away."

"They don't need to go away. You give them something to eat."

I then read the account in Matthew 14:15-21 from The Passion

Translation:

> [15] *Later that afternoon the disciples came to Jesus and said, "It's going to be dark soon and the people are hungry, but there's nothing to eat here in this desolate place. You should send the crowds away to the nearby villages to buy themselves some food."*
>
> [16] *"They don't need to leave," Jesus responded.* ***"You can give them something to eat."***
>
> [17] *They answered, "But all we have is five barley loaves and two fish."*
>
> [18] *"Let me have them," Jesus replied.*
>
> [19] *Then he had everyone sit down on the grass as he took the five loaves and two fish. He looked up into heaven, gave thanks to God, and broke the bread into pieces. He then gave it to his disciples, who in turn gave it to the crowds.*
>
> [20] *And everyone ate until they were satisfied, for the food was multiplied in front of their eyes! They picked up the leftovers and filled up twelve baskets full!* [21] *There were about five thousand men who were fed, in addition to many women and children!* (Emphasis is mine).

I also read the passage in other translations, and verse nineteen of the New King James Version revealed that in giving thanks to the Father, Jesus also blessed the five loaves and two fish that had been given to Him: "*…And He took the five loaves and the two fish, and looking up to heaven, He blessed and broke and gave the loaves to the disciples…*"

He blessed, broke, gave, and a miracle of multiplication followed. Over five thousand (men, plus women and children) were fed, with twelve baskets left over to feed many more!

I had a deep sense of identification with the picture of the hungry multitude, as I also lived with a blessing hunger for most of my life. It was not until 2004 that my hunger was miraculously satisfied. The Holy Spirit had graciously administered the miracle as I pronounced blessings over my life from the book, *The Power of Blessing*, by Terry and Melissa Bone.

The miracle was too good to keep to myself and ever since this turning point in my life, I started to give away what I had received. Many have had their blessing hunger gloriously satisfied. Still, there are more than enough "baskets" left to feed hungry multitudes everywhere.

He

blessed,

broke,

gave,

and a miracle of

multiplication

followed.

Chapter 2

Blessing Multiplication

"In blessing I will bless you..."
— Genesis 22:17 AMPC

Think about it—God blessing us as we bless others! We are the seed of Abraham through faith in Christ Jesus. This promise that God made to Abraham is also ours. Time and again, God has fulfilled this promise in my life. I can't help being blessed as I bless others because it is the Genesis 22:17 principle or "law" of blessing.

Part of my blessing has been the privilege of seeing the blessing multiply as I pass it on to others and savoring the joy it brings to them. I have seen the culture of blessing spring up as more individuals included it in their celebration events. I have seen baby showers, baby dedications, birthdays, weddings, anniversaries, graduations, and ceremonies for seniors transformed by verbal blessings. Beyond that, these blessing impartations have served as a seedbed of inspiration leading others to say, "I want that too."

The Scope of Our Blessing Birthright

In my own life, I have received from the Lord the grace for increase in my anointing and authority to impart the blessing. Revelation concerning our blessing birthright also increased. I had already understood that the blessing God spoke to Adam was a design of the family blessing birthright He intended for us to receive. A further unveiling came through the ministry of Arthur Burk. The Holy Spirit enhanced my understanding to see that we are designed to not only receive spoken blessings, but also to speak blessings over people, places and things. That is what God did on the fifth, sixth and seventh days of creation. We are created to operate like Him and it is part of our fundamental blessing birthright. You will read more about this in Chapter Five.

I came to realize how urgent and important it is for us to be equipped and empowered to operate in this dimension of our birthright that had largely been overlooked. This resource is my response. It is my "five loaves and two fish." In the hands of the Lord and with His blessing, it will multiply and feed hungry multitudes as we distribute the blessing in His authority. I believe that as this resource helps us to possess our baseline birthright blessings, we will be better prepared to possess other birthright treasures that are uniquely ours, individually and as part of a generational legacy.

Mantle Multiplication

Another important purpose this resource serves is to facilitate the impartation of the blessing mantle to others. God is passionate about multiplying the blessing mantle in this season, and He is looking for those who will say "yes" to His call to be a blessing ambassador. Is that you? If it is, ask the Holy Spirit to administer the impartation as you prayerfully read The Blessing Mantle in Appendix One.

My prayer is that you will receive the impartation and be deployed to fulfill your blessing birthright. Do not consider the insufficiency of your ability. Follow the principles that Jesus demonstrated in the feeding of the five thousand:

- Give thanks for the measure of understanding, anointing and authority that you presently have. As Jesus said, "For whoever has, to him more will be given, and he will have abundance" (Matthew 13:12a).

- Bless what you have by invoking God's presence upon it.
- Break it by speaking words that release God's miraculous power.
- Distribute this life-transforming power to your "hungry multitude" and into the culture around you.

Full Redemption of Your Lost Birthright

Jesus has fully redeemed your lost birthright, and it is through your relationship with Him that you will fully experience the joy of supernatural restoration.

How is your relationship with Jesus? If you are not presently enjoying a personal relationship with Him, I invite you to pray this short prayer from a sincere heart:

Heavenly Father, I acknowledge that I have missed the mark you designed for my life. I ask your forgiveness and open my heart now to receive Jesus Christ as my Savior and Lord. Amen.

Congratulations! You have entered into the most important relationship you could ever have; you have received the gift of new life in Jesus Christ, and you are restored to the heart of your heavenly Father.

Your redeemed family blessings are waiting for you; they are in the intangible spiritual realm waiting to be brought into the tangible realm of the earth.

> *Every spiritual blessing in the heavenly realm has already been lavished upon us as a love gift from our wonderful heavenly Father, the Father of our Lord Jesus—all because he sees us wrapped into Christ. This is why we celebrate him with all our hearts!* (Ephesians 1:3 TPT).

Moreover, the authority to operate in your blessing birthright has been

I can't help being
blessed
as I
bless
others... it's a
principle!

given to you by the Father who has raised you up with Christ and seated you together with Him in the heavenly realm.

> *But God still loved us with such great love. He is so rich in compassion and mercy. Even when we were dead and doomed in our many sins, he united us into the very life of Christ and saved us by his wonderful grace! He raised us up with Christ the exalted One, and we ascended with him into the glorious perfection and authority of the heavenly realm, for we are now co-seated as one with Christ!* (Ephesians 2:4-6 TPT).

The Father has graciously put everything in place for you to be blessed and to become an instrument of blessing.

It's too good to keep to yourself. Freely you have received, freely give!

Be blessed as you pay it forward!

Chapter 3

Discovering that Words Matter

Our blessing birthright is essentially the privilege of receiving and giving the gift of words that carry spiritual authority for transformation. Since it was my heavenly Father's plan to ignite the passion of being a blessing ambassador in me, He had to first enlighten me about words, redeem me out of my misconceptions, and heal past wounds.

I was well into my forties when I began to develop an appreciation for the value and power of words as spiritual currency. Up until that time, I did not think that words had any purpose other than being building blocks of communication. It was revolutionary to learn that my words have creative power and could shape my life positively or negatively. It was shocking to discover as well that the words others spoke to me or about me had similar power.

Proverbs 18:21 initiated my awakening: "Death and life are in the power of the tongue." As the unveiling progressed, I realized that my spirit and emotions had already known for a long time what had taken me years to grasp at the intellectual or mental level. I reflected on the jingle I had heard and said many times as a young girl: "Sticks and stones may break my bones, but words will never hurt me."

Although I had bought into this lie and had given mental assent to it, at a deeper level, my spirit knew otherwise. Now in this season of enlightenment, I courageously faced the truth—*words do hurt*. In fact, I discovered in Proverbs 12:18 that their injuries pierce like a sword. Words (mine and those of others) had hurt me and produced undesirable fruit in my life. Regrettably, I had likely also hurt others with my words.

Healing the Past through Repentance and Forgiveness

To no avail I spent much time wishing I had known and done better. However, the past can never be wished away. Eventually I pushed beyond wishing. With faith in the blood of Jesus that purchased my forgiveness at the Cross, I clung to the promise of God that "if we confess our sins, He is faithful and just to forgive us of our sins and cleanse us from all unrighteousness" (1 John 1:9).

I repented of my "ab-use" (*ab*-normal *use*) of words. I received forgiveness and released myself and others from the consequences and effects of my ill-spoken words. It was not just a one-time thing. As the Holy Spirit reminded me of situations, I found grace to repeat the process. I also forgave and released myself from the unhealthy words that others had spoken over me. I am ever so grateful for the grace of God that leads us to repentance, grants forgiveness and gives us a new beginning.

My New Beginning

My eyes were opened to see the creation account in a new way. I found my new beginning *in the beginning*. I had heard and read the creation account in Genesis many times before. Yet, it had never really dawned on me that words were the instrument that God used to bring forth, fashion, shape and order all of creation. I received the revelation from Hebrews 11:3—"By faith we understand that the worlds were framed by the word of God, so that the things which are seen were not made of things which are visible."

In discovering the creative power of words, I experienced the truth of Romans 8:28 at a personal level: "And we know that all things work

Words are
building blocks,
not only for a good sentence,
but for a
good life.

together for good to those who love God, to those who are the called according to His purpose." I became passionate about the wisdom of using our words for good. I gradually became what I call a "word watcher"—watching my words and encouraging others to do the same.

I later discovered the generational impact of words. "Spoken words are like the fruit of a tree—of either blessing or cursing—that either nourishes or poisons future generations."[3] In delivering myself from the consequences of a "cursing tongue," I was creating the legacy of a "blessing tongue" for present and future generations.

Principles and Passages for a New Mindset

The following principles and passages, among others, were instrumental in realigning the thoughts and feelings of my heart, so I could have a new mindset, new respect for words, and a new tongue:

- I am created in the image and likeness of God to operate like Him and to represent Him on earth. I, therefore, have the privilege of collaborating with Him by expressing His power, authority and love in the words I speak, especially the Word that He gives me for specific persons, places and things.

- Jesus (the Word at the beginning)[4] took on human form so that I could be brought into the right relationship with Himself (the Living Word). He restored my ability to hear and speak the words of the Father, and to release His Spirit-life through my words.

- God's Word incubated in my spirit is my richest treasure and most valuable resource.

- Words are building blocks, not only for a good sentence, but for a good life.

- Words are like seeds that germinate and produce either positive or negative substance. They reproduce after their kind, which means, we will have what we say.

- I am divinely designed to use my words as a creative and transformative force to change lives and circumstances.
- Words are containers and conveyors. I have the power to choose words that convey the blessings of the Father.

- May the words of my mouth and the meditation of my heart be pleasing to you, O Lord, my rock and my redeemer (Psalm 19:14 NLT).
- And never let ugly or hateful words come from your mouth, but instead let your words become beautiful gifts that encourage others; do this by speaking words of grace to help them (Ephesians 4:29 TPT).
- Let your speech always be with grace, seasoned with salt, that you may know how you ought to answer each one (Colossians 4:6).
- Like apples of gold in settings of silver, so is a word skillfully spoken (Proverbs 25:11 NET).
- The tongue of the righteous is choice silver…The lips of the righteous feed many (Proverbs 10:20a, 21a).
- The words of the wise soothe and heal (Proverbs 12:18b TPT).
- Sharing words of wisdom is satisfying to your inner being. It encourages you to know that you've changed someone else's life. Your words are so powerful that they will kill or give life (Proverbs 18:20-21a TPT).

- When you speak healing words, you offer others fruit from the tree of life (Proverbs 15:4a TPT).
- Your word I have hidden in my heart that I might not sin against You (Psalm 119:11).

Little did I know, that this journey of discovering the power and value of words was a stepping stone. It became the precursor to the defining moment when I would discover the spiritual art of crafting words as blessings of transformation. Gradually, and by God's grace, my tongue became "the pen of a ready writer"[5] to write wholesome words on my own heart and the hearts of others.

Your Personal Checkup

I encourage you to spend some time in the presence of the Holy Spirit examining your mindset about words and how you use them. Ask the Holy Spirit to take you through the process of healing and do any necessary realignment. Repentance for having missed the mark will release to you the grace for a new beginning as it did for me.

Chapter 4

Defining Moments of 2004

Eureka! For many years, the word "eureka" topped my list of favorites. My sister attended a preparatory school by that name in our community in May Pen, Jamaica, and I found the word quite intriguing. I eventually learned that it meant: *I have found it!*

The word perfectly captures an experience I had in August 2004. Borrowing the Merriam-Webster definition, what happened that summer was "a moment of sudden, triumphant discovery, inspiration or insight." The moment began with the gift of a book. A dear friend had seen the newly published book by Terry and Melissa Bone, *The Power of Blessing*, on a television broadcast and ordered it for me. I received my copy on the first day of August and on that same day, I started a journey that transformed my life forever. A whole new world unfolded. Revelation-light illuminated each page and fountains of tears that I did not know I had in me, rushed out through new pathways.

Finding My Lost Birthright

The discovery was exhilarating and disheartening all at once; I had a birthright that I had not yet received! God had designed for me to receive spoken blessings at pivotal stages of my life, starting from conception, and I did not get them. The book referred to this birthright as the "Family Blessing." Up to that point, the only blessings I knew of were those I had read about in Deuteronomy 28, as a reward for walking in obedience to God's law under the Old Covenant. However, I didn't think I really qualified for them. The discovery that there was a kind of blessing for which I qualified, just for being born, was nothing short of exhilarating!

From the authors' description of the Family Blessing, their illustrations taken from the early life of Jesus and other stories, I felt as if I had struck gold. I had found that mysterious, missing "something." It was the key to my having an unshakeable sense of belonging, love, dignity, value, and significance. Their description of the Family Blessing provided word pictures that I related to in a big way: "Words, deeds and ceremonies [that] confer heaven's favor upon our identity and destiny...with them we prosper despite our weaknesses. Without them we struggle even though we may be gifted."[6]

I saw that the blessing which God imparted to Adam in Genesis 1:28, was the "prototype" of this foundational or fundamental birthright blessing. In blessing Adam, the heavenly Father was modelling His intent for His entire family of human offspring to have blessings pronounced upon their identity and destiny. Following the ancient patriarchs, the Jewish culture has preserved this wonderful treasure of spoken blessings; but it isn't so for many other people groups. The reality is that most families have missed it. Mine certainly did.

The comforting presence of the Holy Spirit overshadowed my sense of loss and caused me to latch on to the authors' conviction— "It's never too late to recover missed blessings or pass them along to the next generation." What amazing grace!

Recovering the Blessings I had Missed

In reading through the seven life stages and related questions that the authors had developed,[7] and upon evaluating my own experience, I determined that I had a huge blessing deficit. Here I was, at my sixth "border crossing" (adulthood) and I needed the full deposit of blessing for each of the five previous life stages.

There is a kind of *blessing*
for which you *qualified*,
just for being *born*.

An echo in my spirit reassured me, "You can catch up."

Ephesians 1:3 shone as a bright beacon of hope; "Blessed be the God and Father of our Lord Jesus Christ, who has blessed us with every spiritual blessing in the heavenly places in Christ." I could recover what I missed because of what Jesus had accomplished in His finished work of redemption. My missed blessings were not lost forever!

Faith transported me through the timeline of my life, latched onto the blessings stored up in the heavenly places in Christ, pulled them down and deposited them in my heart. It was a massive supernatural recovery operation as I pronounced blessing after blessing on myself for each major life-stage—at conception, in the womb, at my birth, through infancy and childhood, over my teen years, and now in adulthood.

An Instant Blessing Distributor

Catching up on my missed blessings released a tangible wave of healing from my inside out, and the miracle was much too good to keep to myself. As the disciples had done in the feeding of the five thousand, I immediately started "distributing" what I had received from the Lord.

My husband was the first recipient. The occasion was our twenty-seventh wedding anniversary on the sixth of August 2004. Although it was only five days since I had received the book, my blessing cup was sufficiently filled for him to drink from my overflow. He was pleasantly surprised and joyfully received my gift of intentional words that honored him as a husband and blessed our marriage.

Other family members and friends also received their portion as their birthdays and other special events came around. My Dad, who was living in Jamaica, had his blessing transmitted to him by way of a long-distance phone call. What a privilege it was to rise and call him blessed, to bestow honor on him for his life's work, and to convey the heavenly Father's heart of love to him. Given the cultural milieu in which he was raised, I knew this was the first time he had encountered affirming love in this way. He thanked me profusely.

Receiving the Blessing Mantle

Before the year ended, the Lord engineered an opportunity for me to share with Terry Bone my testimony of the transformation that the blessing had brought to me and others through his book. I was surprised when he asked permission to record my testimony for the DVD product he was developing. Little did I know that I was in for an even bigger surprise!

The recording session was in February of 2005. At the end of the session, Pastor Terry announced that the Holy Spirit had instructed him to impart the blessing mantle to me. He did!

This autographed blessing that he wrote on behalf of Melissa and himself sealed the impartation:
"*May the Lord anoint you to bring the message of blessing to many!*
Terry and Melissa Bone
Ephesians 1:3
February 2005"

Chapter 5

Defining Moments of 2017

Thirteen years had gone by since 2004 when I recovered my missed blessing. Thousands of words had been crafted into verbal and written blessings. The message had been delivered wherever the Lord gave me an open door, with no one and no venue being off limits: from kitchens, dining rooms and living rooms to elegant banquet halls; at conferences, church and community gatherings of all sizes, in nursing homes, on television programs, and by telephone.

My experiences in 2017 resembled answers to the prayer of Jabez: "Oh, that You would bless me indeed, and enlarge my territory, that Your hand would be with me, and that You would keep me from evil, that I may not cause pain!" (1 Chronicles 4:10). God's grace had kept me from the temptation to hold back and lay aside my blessing mantle until I felt better equipped. Out of the awkward, small beginnings, the hand of God brought forth increase—enlarged territory.

Babies in the womb received welcome blessings before seeing the light of day. The blessing even made its way to prison inmates. The elderly, the young, and the not so young all traversed time to possess their missing birthright treasures. Invitations for blessing impartations at weddings, graduation and ordination services, and events with community dignitaries broadened the scope and variety beyond my expectation. This enlargement of my "blessing territory" attested to the faithfulness of God and His passion to see the culture of blessing restored.

New Dimensions Unveiled

The year 2017 brought much revelation concerning the blessing. By divinely engineered circumstances, a colleague introduced me to a teaching album by Arthur Burk on *Ministering to Babies in the Womb.* This resource supplied the missing pieces of the puzzle for the parenting model I had been building for the "conception-to-age-two" period. The generosity of our God never fails to overwhelm me. God had given me a two-for-one deal. The resource not only provided the missing pieces for the parenting project, it also unveiled new dimensions of our blessing birthright from the creation account in Genesis.

As you will read in the summary that follows, the main areas of unveiling related to our three-fold birthright, the three kinds of spoken blessings, and engaging the human spirit.

We have a three-fold birthright as God's image bearers. It was already part of my faith foundation that God created us in His image and likeness to operate just as He did. The unveiling of the three main capacities in which God operated at creation was new: (1) He created, (2) He established social order, and (3) He spoke blessing. Humanity has become proficient in the first two areas of operation—we are makers and inventors, and we are adept at organizing social structures. However, the area of speaking blessing has been largely neglected. In this unpacking of the creation account, I discovered that our God-given authority to speak words of blessing extended over people, places and things.

Against the escalating evil of our times, this revelation of the neglected dimension of our birthright gave me a deep sense of urgency. I saw that in speaking blessings like our Creator God, we had a divine strategy for making pre-emptive strikes against evil. Through the instrument of blessing, we had the opportunity to shift our energy from the defensive posture of breaking curses to concentrate on the offensive strategy of releasing God's presence, power and authority to establish His intent on the earth.

Three prototypes of spoken blessings. Further unpacking of the creation account ensued. I realized for the first time that God spoke three different kinds of blessings on three of the seven days of creation: (1) blessing of design (identity and destiny) on the fifth day, (2) blessing of authority, dominion and provision to Adam on the sixth day, and (3) blessing of the consecration of time on the seventh day.

This new understanding allowed me to receive grace for an enlarged blessing mantle, especially for the blessing of consecration. Up until that point, I had been passionate about blessing people. Now, the Lord had opened my eyes to see that places and things were also under the full purview of the spoken blessing. I sensed that I had connected with God's supernatural key to transform our culture by releasing the power of blessing into its various spheres.

Engaging our human spirit. I was aware that according to God's design, humans are three-dimensional beings of spirit, soul, and body, with the spirit designed to lead. However, the concept of engaging the human spirit was brand new. My theology had focused so heavily on the Holy Spirit that I had given little or no conscious attention to my human spirit which shared the same essence as God's. Yet, God had designed my spirit to lead my soul and body through active cooperation with the Holy Spirit. I began to recognize the longing of the Holy Spirit for my spirit to become more consciously and actively engaged with Him. Furthermore, I was delighted to learn that there is no competition between my spirit and the Holy Spirit.

The "Aha" moment came when I discovered that engaging a person's spirit for a blessing impartation made the delivery and reception much more powerful. I got it. We could say that verbal blessing is a "spirit thing"—a spiritual reality, and it targets the human spirit because we receive and interpret spiritual truths with spiritual faculties.[8]

For the most part, even after being born again, our human spirit remains marginalized as we are not taught how to nurture, nourish or engage our spirit.[9] This revelation of engaging spirit-to-spirit has greatly impacted how I minister the blessing.

The first time I intentionally ministered spirit-to-spirit in a blessing impartation was with a group of youth and young adults. What a difference it made to invite their spirit to come forward to receive the blessing. The Holy Spirit was present to facilitate this impartation. The expression on the faces of many of these young people spoke volumes about what they had experienced. We had undoubtedly engaged at a spirit-to-spirit level.

This revelation boosted my faith with great expectations for the outcome of ministry to babies in the womb and to infants. With the human spirit being most alert in these early stages of development, they are the optimum seasons for nurturing the spirit with spoken blessings.

The Hallmark of the Year

I was preparing to minister at a women's conference when the Holy Spirit gave me the crowning revelation of the year: *I will show you how the fruit of the Spirit[10] relates to the seven life stages of the family blessing.* His instruction was to wait in His presence and write out the blessing to give to the women rather than do an impromptu impartation as I had done many times before. He graciously poured into me the words of blessing for each of the seven life stages and showed me the fruit of the Spirit connection for each stage. (The chart in Appendix Two shows the connections).

I received two additional instructions:

1. Read the blessing verbatim so as not to miss the precise words He had given me.
2. Engage the women in a practical exercise to intentionally plant the fruit of the Spirit in their heart at each stage.

For the practical exercise, I typed the word for each fruit of the Spirit (love, joy, peace, patience, kindness, goodness, faithfulness, gentleness, self-control) on a piece of paper and put it in a small envelope. I had an envelope for each participant and instructed them to remove all nine pieces of paper. At the end of the blessing impartation for each life-stage, they were to insert the "fruit(s)" applicable to that stage in the envelope. I informed them that the envelope represented their heart, and with this action they were creating supernatural synergy between the fruit of the Spirit and the words of blessing that had been deposited in their heart. I later learned that one participant took her envelope to work the following week and laid out the pieces of paper on her desk as a visual reminder and reinforcement of her experience of transformation.

During this first "clinic," the presence of the Holy Spirit was more tangible than I had ever experienced during a blessing impartation. The Holy Spirit had found a conducive atmosphere—I had intentionally engaged the spirit of the women and He (Holy Spirit) had our full cooperation.

I had found golden keys for the impartation of blessings to others at all ages and stages of life. The blessing impartation you will receive in Part Two captures these new-found treasures.

This momentous occasion of October 2017 marked the birth of the

Blessing Recovery Clinic. You will have an opportunity to participate in the "clinic" in Part Two.

Speaking blessings
is a divine strategy for making
pre-emptive strikes
against evil.

Chapter 6

Worth Its Weight in Gold

Can you imagine a future where silence does not leave children to figure out who they really are and their purpose for being alive? A future where deep wounds inflicted by ill-spoken words are not left to fester and later erupt into emotional and physical violence? Can you imagine a future in which spoken blessing is the mainstay of our lives from the womb to the end of our days? Can you imagine a future where we live in a culture saturated with the power of blessing, where we walk in the authority of our God-given blessing birthright and not just bless our food before we eat, or say "God bless you" when a person sneezes?

It is possible!

We could call this the "hope chapter" of the book because it answers our questions loud and clear— "Yes!" such a future is indeed possible; we only need to be intentional about creating it.

Esau and Jacob, the twin sons of Isaac, are the focus of this chapter. Their stories help us to get a deeper understanding of the value of the spoken blessing and its significance in Jewish culture from ancient times up to the present.

We first meet the twins in Genesis 25 when their mother, Rebekah, inquired of the Lord about the jostling of the babies in her womb. Esau was born first, with the hand of Jacob grasping his heel. According to the tradition, the enviable double portion inheritance belonged to Esau as the firstborn. However, one day, Esau came home famished after a hard day of hunting and succumbed to Jacob's cunning offer that stripped him of his birthright. Esau bartered his birthright for a serving of lentil stew. Genesis 25 ends with these very sad words: "So Esau despised his birthright."

A couple of chapters later, we meet Esau again in Genesis 27. This time, his blind, aged, dying father is giving him instructions to prepare for the impartation of his long-awaited firstborn blessing. Rebekah overheard Isaac's instructions to Esau: "...Prepare me the kind of tasty food I like and bring it to me to eat, so that I may give you my blessing before I die." Since Jacob was Rebekah's favorite son, she intercepted the plan so that he (Jacob) could receive the blessing instead. She quickly devised a scheme for Jacob to disguise himself as Esau, take food to his father, and get the double portion birthright blessing which was customarily reserved for the firstborn.

Let's pick up the story after Jacob had successfully executed the plot:

> 30 *After Isaac finished blessing him, and Jacob had scarcely left his father's presence, his brother Esau came in from hunting.*
>
> 31 *He too prepared some tasty food and brought it to his father. Then he said to him, "My father, please sit up and eat some of my game, so that you may give me your blessing."*
>
> 32 *His father Isaac asked him, "Who are you?"*
>
> *"I am your son," he answered, "your firstborn, Esau."*
>
> 33 *Isaac trembled violently and said, "Who was it, then, that hunted game and brought it to me? I ate it just before you came and I blessed him—and indeed he will be blessed!"*
>
> 34 *When Esau heard his father's words,* ***he burst out with a loud and bitter cry and said to his father, "Bless me—me too, my father!"***

35 But he said, "Your brother came deceitfully and took your blessing."

36 Esau said, "Isn't he rightly named Jacob? This is the second time he has taken advantage of me: He took my birthright, and now he's taken my blessing!" Then he asked, "Haven't you reserved any blessing for me?"

37 Isaac answered Esau, "I have made him lord over you and have made all his relatives his servants, and I have sustained him with grain and new wine. So what can I possibly do for you, my son?"

38 Esau said to his father, "Do you have only one blessing, my father? ***Bless me too, my father!" Then Esau wept aloud.***

39 His father Isaac answered him, "Your dwelling will be away from the earth's richness, away from the dew of heaven above.

40 You will live by the sword and you will serve your brother. But when you grow restless, you will throw his yoke from off your neck."

41 Esau held a grudge against Jacob because of the blessing his father had given him. He said to himself, "The days of mourning for my father are near; then I will kill my brother Jacob" (Genesis 27: 1-4; 30-41 NIV, emphasis is mine).

What is it About the Blessing?

Esau's heart wrenching cry echoes in my ear every time I read this story. Prior to understanding as much as I do now about the blessing, I had two questions:

- What is it about a verbal blessing that could have caused Rebekah and Jacob to engage in such trickery?
- What is it about a verbal blessing that could have caused a grown

man at the age of forty to weep so bitterly because words intended for him were spoken to his brother instead?

Thinking back to the first brothers in human history, Cain and Abel, and what I have come to know so well about family relationships, I thought I had the answer—sibling rivalry. Then one day, about ten years ago, I realized the issue was much deeper. I was listening to a teaching by Dr. Ed Montgomery of Abundant Life Cathedral on *The Blessing Factor*; in it he made this profound statement: "In ancient times the most coveted thing was not wealth or power. It was the blessing, because whoever possessed the blessing possessed it all." I got the explanation for Esau's heart-rending response!

There is a supernatural authority inherent in the blessing that is designed by God to empower and thrust us into our God-given identity and destiny. "With them [blessings] we prosper despite our weaknesses. Without them we struggle even though we may be gifted."[11]

Bless Me—Me too!

We are made for the blessing and everything that God designed it to convey—love, dignity, legitimacy, honor, value, significance, empowerment, favor and so much more. When the blessing is missed or lost, the cry of every person's heart is the same as that of Esau's: *Bless me—me too*!

Whether the cry is at the conscious or subconscious level, it is a deep consuming force that eventually finds expression in debilitating emotions and behaviors. The absence of the blessing amounts to a "silent rejection," especially when hurtful words and emotional abuse take the place that the blessing was meant to fill.

Our own lives as well as the findings of clinicians, counsellors, pastors and others, attest to the sense of shame and worthlessness, arrested development, underperformance, overperformance, fear, hate, depression, anger, violence, and a host of other maladies that manifest from various forms of rejection. Still, there is hope to be found in the freedom, restoration, healing and wholeness that God designed the spoken blessing to convey.

Jacob's Legacy of Blessing

We are grateful for God's redemptive mercy in the life of Jacob. He eventually transformed Jacob from a deceiver into a patriarch through whom He could fulfill the blessing promises that He had made to Abraham for the benefit of all humanity:

- *I will bless you...And you shall be a blessing...And in you all the families of the earth shall be blessed* (Genesis 12:2-3).
- *In blessing I will bless thee* (Genesis 22:17 KJV).

More than anyone else, Jacob understood the power and value of the spoken blessing. First, he stole his brother's blessing, and then he later wrestled with God for a blessing.

> [24] *Then Jacob was left alone; and a Man wrestled with him until the breaking of day.*
>
> [25] *Now when He saw that He did not prevail against him, He touched the socket of his hip; and the socket of Jacob's hip was out of joint as He wrestled with him.*
>
> [26] *And He said, "Let Me go, for the day breaks." But he said,* ***"I will not let You go unless You bless me!"***
>
> [27] *So He said to him, "What is your name?" He said, "Jacob."*
>
> [28] *And He said, "Your name shall no longer be called Jacob, but Israel; for you have struggled with God and with men, and have*

> *prevailed."*
>
> 29 *Then Jacob asked, saying, "Tell me Your name, I pray." And He said, "Why is it that you ask about My name?" And He blessed him there* (Genesis 32:24-29, emphasis is mine).

We are not surprised that it was Jacob who eventually established the unshakeable legacy of blessing which remains at the heart of Jewish culture even to this day. He did this through his two grandsons who were born to Joseph in Egypt. Joseph had named the firstborn son Manasseh, which means "making forgetful," and the second son, he named Ephraim, which means "fruitfulness" (see Genesis 41:50-52).

In Genesis 48, we read how Jacob sovereignly placed his right hand upon the head of Ephraim, although it should have been on Manasseh, the firstborn. When Joseph tried to correct his father, Jacob persisted. He repeated the pattern of what had transpired in his own life—the younger son receiving the greater blessing that customarily would have been bestowed on the firstborn.

> 18 *And Joseph said to his father, "Not so, my father, for this one is the firstborn; put your right hand on his head."*
>
> 19 *But his father refused and said, "I know, my son, I know. He also shall become a people, and he also shall be great; but truly his younger brother shall be greater than he, and his descendants shall become a multitude of nations."*
>
> 20 *So he blessed them that day, saying, "By you Israel will bless, saying, 'May God make you as Ephraim and as Manasseh!'" And thus he set Ephraim before Manasseh* (Genesis 48:18-20).

God is sovereign. Here we see Him defying custom to establish His eternal plan. Although Esau and Manasseh were both firstborns, God sovereignly chose to work through Jacob and Ephraim, both second-born, in fulfilling His covenant promises to Abraham.

A Success Key

People marvel at the success of the Jewish people, much of which can be attributed to the significant role verbal blessings have played in their lives throughout the generations. They believe the promises of blessing God gave to their forefather Abraham, and they have clung passionately to the legacy established by Jacob in the blessing of Joseph's two sons, Ephraim and Manasseh:

> *By you Israel will bless, saying, 'May God make you as Ephraim and as Manasseh!'* (Genesis 48:20).

Orthodox Jewish families have not ceased to bless their children with these powerful words week after week during their Friday evening Shabbat (Sabbath) ceremony: "May God make you like Ephraim and Manasseh." Sometimes the blessing incorporates the meaning of the names— "making forgetful" and "fruitfulness:"

> *May you be like Ephraim and Manasseh—may you forget the pain of your past and may you bear much fruit in your future.*[12]

Can you imagine hearing these words on a regular basis? Weekly? Add it all up, and perhaps, this is the secret to the overall success of the Jewish people and their collective contribution to the welfare of humanity, especially in scientific and medical discoveries: "In an observant Jewish family, most children receive a personal blessing nearly a thousand times before they leave their parents' home."[13] The blessings do not stop when they leave home. Since verbal blessings are in their DNA and a normal way of life, most adult children continue the lifestyle of blessing when they leave home and start their own families.

The language of the Ephraim and Manasseh blessing is proactive and remedial. On the proactive side, it imprints a safeguard against strife and relational trauma since these two brothers were the first in recorded biblical history to live without rivalry. Jewish children are raised to emulate their example and develop a mindset for living harmoniously and working together for the benefit of the larger community.

The remedial component of this blessing is phenomenal for several reasons. I want to highlight two of them. In the first place, the regular impartation of this trans-generational blessing, continuously neutralizes the horrific pain and trauma that was inflicted upon the Jewish people at different times in history. It is not too late for other people groups that have suffered atrocities to tap into this potent, supernatural solution. The blessing was meant for all people groups because God's promise to Abraham was that "in you all the families of the earth shall be blessed" (Genesis 12:3b).

Secondly, despite noble intentions, the dynamics of family life and human relationships generally are such that children can and do sustain emotional wounds, even from parents. Although the hurt is sometimes unintentional and accidental, it still causes damage. Every people group and every family need an antidote and where one does not exist, the pain accumulates and festers.

In their customary Ephraim and Manasseh blessing, the Jewish people have the antidote for childhood family traumas and other kinds as well. Aaron Früh sums up the benefit in this way: "Every father who continues this practice is speaking by faith that his children will forget the pain of their past and bear fruit in their future."[14] It makes sense then that the Jewish people are, generally speaking, the most fruitful in the world.

Shabbat blessings include the singing or speaking of the "Sabbath Blessing" from the movie, *Fiddler on the Roof* over all the children (see Appendix Three). Daughters receive a special blessing as well. In the

It is not too late
to tap into this
potent,
supernatural
solution.

customary blessing for daughters, the pronouncement is: "May God make you like the Mothers of Israel, even Sarah, Rebekah, Rachel and Leah." These are the women through whom God worked to produce the patriarchal leaders of the twelve tribes.

In the blessing of the daughters, as in the blessing of the sons, the imprint left in the spirit, heart and soul of each child is altruism, not selfishness. A genuine concern for the welfare of others is desperately needed in today's society, and through verbal blessings, all families can sow seeds that will bear similar fruit now and in generations to come.

In addition to these blessings, both the Father at home and the Rabbi after every service in the Synagogue, declare the Aaronic priestly blessing over everyone:

> *The Lord bless you and keep you: The Lord make his face to shine upon you, and be gracious to you. The Lord lift up his countenance upon you, and give you peace* (Numbers 6:24-26).

I am not suggesting that the Jewish people and their culture are flawless. They do, however, have the well-established cultural heritage of the spoken blessing that could make a big difference for children everywhere.

God's Ancient Path

The way of blessing is one of God's ancient paths. He longs for us to return to His pathway and experience its benefits of healing, restoration, and protection. The prophet Jeremiah records God's appeal that is relevant to us today:

> *This is what the LORD says: Stand at the crossroads and look; ask for the ancient paths, ask where the good way is, and walk in it, and you will find rest for your souls. But you said, 'We will not walk in it'* (Jeremiah 6:16 NIV).

In Jeremiah's time, the people refused. My prayer is that we would be a generation and a people who will respond to the loving appeal of our God.

Can You Imagine?

Once more, let me ask one of the questions I started with: Can you imagine not just a future, but a near future in which spoken blessing is the mainstay of our lives, all the way from the womb to the end of our days?

We are those called by God to partner with Him in creating such a future. He is ready to release His mantle of authority upon all who will answer the call to be a blessing ambassador.

Chapter 7

Blessing Ambassadors

Are you ready for God's mantle? The purpose of this special mantle is to see the power of God's glory released through spoken blessings to transform our lives, the lives of others, and our culture. I believe you have pressed through this far because your heart is responding to the Father's heart. I bless your perseverance and welcome you into partnership with God for this calling as a blessing ambassador.

Knowing who you are called to be and what you are called to do as a blessing ambassador are of utmost importance. This chapter will help to build a good foundation by drawing heavily on the Scriptures, especially the Apostle Paul's letter to the Ephesians. His letter unveils significant truths that are relevant to your receiving and pronouncing spoken blessings as well as operating in the mantle and authority of a blessing ambassador.

You will notice that most of the Bible passages cited in this chapter are taken from The Passion Translation (TPT) and The Voice Translation. This is because of how important it is to grasp the message that the passages convey. Reading Scripture in unfamiliar language somehow moves us beyond what we know intellectually and engages our spirit for more revelation-light.

Insights from Ephesians

The blessing is available and ready for distribution: You and those to whom you will impart spoken blessings have already been blessed by our wonderful heavenly Father. It is on the strength of this truth that we receive and give the blessing by faith. We are eternally grateful to our Lord Jesus for redeeming all that we had lost in Adam.

> *Every spiritual blessing in the heavenly realm has already been lavished upon us as a love gift from our wonderful heavenly Father, the Father of our Lord Jesus—all because he sees us wrapped into Christ* (Ephesians 1:3 TPT).

Here is another critical verse from the Apostle Paul's letter to the Galatians:

> *Jesus, our Messiah, was cursed in our place and in so doing, dissolved the curse from our lives, so that all the blessings of Abraham can be poured out upon even non-Jewish believers. And now God gives us the promise of the wonderful Holy Spirit who lives within us when we believe in him* (Galatians 3:14 TPT).

Your riches, calling, and power: As blessing ambassadors, we need to be sustained by a vision larger than ourselves, and the Apostle Paul has prayed for us to see beyond ourselves. His prayer helps us to see that the Father of glory has endowed us with His riches, called us, and empowered us to build a legacy that transforms lives and culture. We can do it—one blessing at a time. You are encouraged to personalize the prayer and pray it often. I have been doing this for many years and have seen much fruit in my life.

> 17 *I pray that the Father of glory, the God of our Lord Jesus Christ, would impart to you the riches of the Spirit of wisdom and the Spirit of revelation to know him through your deepening intimacy with him.*
>
> 18 *I pray that the light of God will illuminate the eyes of your*

> *imagination, flooding you with light, until you experience the full revelation of the hope of his calling—that is, the wealth of God's glorious inheritances that he finds in us, his holy ones!*
>
> [19] *I pray that you will continually experience the immeasurable greatness of God's power made available to you through faith. Then your lives will be an advertisement of this immense power as it works through you! This is the mighty power.*
>
> [20] *that was released when God raised Christ from the dead and exalted him to the place of highest honor and supreme authority in the heavenly realm!* (Ephesians 1:17-20 TPT).

You have divine authority: Part of your authority as a blessing ambassador comes from your seated position in the heavenly realm in Christ. (Remember that Ephesians 3 tells us that our spiritual blessings are also in the same place!) We are bi-locational beings operating both in the physical and spiritual realms. A consciousness of your spiritual position is fundamental to exercising your delegated authority as a blessing ambassador.

> *He raised us up with Christ the exalted One, and we ascended with him into the glorious perfection and authority of the heavenly realm, for we are now co-seated as one with Christ!* (Ephesians 2:6 TPT).

You are God's masterpiece or poetry: God destined and wonderfully designed you as His masterpiece—His poetry. Poetry has to do with words, correct? You have been crafted with words, so it is part of your intrinsic ability to also craft words into blessing to fulfill your destiny as a blessing ambassador.

> *We have become his poetry, a re-created people that will fulfill the destiny he has given each of us, for we are joined to Jesus, the Anointed One. Even before we were born, God planned in*

> *advance our destiny and the good works we would do to fulfill it!* (Ephesians 2:10 TPT).

The Father's love is your bedrock: The heavenly Father's heart of love is the source of all blessing. As blessing ambassadors, we receive His love and in turn convey it to others. Listen to the prayer of the Apostle Paul for the heavenly Father's love to become the bedrock of your life:

> [16]*Father, out of Your honorable and glorious riches, strengthen Your people. Fill their souls with the power of Your Spirit*
>
> [17]*so that through faith the Anointed One will reside in their hearts. May love be the rich soil where their lives take root. May it be the bedrock where their lives are founded* (Ephesians 3:16-17 Voice).

In Colossians 2:2, he says:

> *I am contending for you that your hearts will be wrapped in the comfort of heaven and woven together into love's fabric. This will give you access to all the riches of God as you experience the revelation of God's great mystery—Christ* (TPT).

May it be so in the Name of Jesus!

Your Identity Blueprint

In the governmental arena, the name "ambassador" reveals much about the person and his/her assignment. The definition from Dictionary.com is, "a diplomatic official of the highest rank, sent by one sovereign or state to another as its resident representative. An authorized representative or messenger." The English Oxford Dictionary adds, "a representative or promoter of a specific activity."

Do you see it? You are sent as an authorized official, messenger, representative, and promoter of a specific activity. What specific activity? To restore the culture of spoken blessing. Your verbal blessings bring heaven to earth and reconcile earth to heaven. Your accreditation from God for this calling is found in 2 Corinthians 5:20— "Now then, we are ambassadors for Christ."

You are a king-priest: A significant facet of your identity as a blessing ambassador relates to the kingly priesthood that Jesus has conferred upon us:

> *And [He] has made us kings and priests to His God and Father…* (Revelation 1:6).
>
> *And have made us kings and priests to our God; And we shall reign on the earth* (Revelation 5:10).
>
> *But you are God's chosen treasure—priests who are kings, a spiritual "nation" set apart as God's devoted ones. He called you out of darkness to experience his marvelous light, and now he claims you as his very own. He did this so that you would broadcast his glorious wonders throughout the world* (1 Peter 2:9 TPT).

God had a specific mandate for the Levitical priesthood, which also applies to you as a New Testament priest:

> *Then the priests, the sons of Levi, shall come near, for the Lord your God has chosen them to minister to Him and to bless in the name of the Lord; by their word every controversy and every assault shall be settled* (Deuteronomy 21:5).

Your words of blessing are a powerful instrument for "settling assaults" of every kind; for releasing individuals out of psychological and spiritual bondage, and to bring about their transformation. Since you pronounce blessings in the name of the Lord, it means that as a priest, your words carry the weight of God's authority in the spiritual realm.

In your kingship identity, your words also carry great power as

Ecclesiastes 8:4 attests: "Where the word of a king is, there is power…" So as a king-priest blessing ambassador, your words are vested with a double portion of speaking power and spiritual authority.

You are a restorer: Being a restorer is another significant aspect of your identity as a blessing ambassador.

> *Those from among you shall build the old waste places; You shall raise up the foundations of many generations; And you shall be called the Repairer of the Breach, The Restorer of Streets to Dwell In* (Isaiah 58:12).

The New Living Translation says, "…you will be known as a rebuilder of walls and a restorer of homes." Individuals, families, homes, and communities all have painful breaches from the past that need to be healed and restored. God wants to use your verbal blessings as a redemptive instrument to heal the gaping wounds inflicted by different forms of abuse, especially verbal abuse.

Parents have an extraordinary, special role. Craig Hill of Family Foundations International puts things into perspective:

> *Whether they realize it or not, parents hold a powerful key to the future lives of their children in blessing and cursing…blessing is God's ordained method of imparting identity and destiny to people, and parents are* ***God's ordained agents*** *through whom this will come. Unfortunately, many of our parents failed to have knowledge of their job description before they became parents. As a result, many of us received the devil's message, by default, throughout most of our growing-up years.*[15] (Emphasis is mine).

Nevertheless, all is not lost, neither is it too late! In the introduction, I had shared Aaron Früh's perspective on verbal abuse. I want to repeat it because of the message of hope it conveys: "It is my premise that much of the iniquity that is passed from generation to generation is a result of verbal abuse. And if that is the case, if it is through the tongue that we were cursed, then **I believe it is through the tongue that blessing and healing will come.**" (Emphasis is mine).

With the riches of God's wisdom filling you, you possess a tongue through which blessing and healing will come. As Proverbs 12:18 says, "…the tongue of the wise brings healing." We begin the cycle of healing and restoration with ourselves, and the Blessing Recovery Clinic in Part Two is designed for this purpose. Recovering our missed blessings puts us in a position to end the circle of brokenness in generations after us. Our words of blessing will nourish and protect them instead. Let's be generous with our gift of life-giving words, because "a person needs five positive messages for every one negative message spoken to them."[16]

Our goal is to shift from remedying negative messages to proactively speak words of blessing. If you are a parent or grandparent, I encourage you to start speaking blessings over your children and grandchildren as early as possible, and to be consistent. The ideal time to start is while the child is in the womb. Early exposure to the blessing and your consistency will cause your children and grandchildren to grow up anticipating your words of blessing. Mary Ruth Swope has written an amazing little book with forty-nine examples, seven weeks' worth of blessings that she spoke to her grandson.[17]

Your Mantle and Authority

God's design and His anointing are your mantle; the weight of His backing is your authority. By God's design, parents and grandparents carry the mantle and authority to pronounce blessings on their children and grandchildren to shape their identity and destiny, and for the transfer of a righteous generational legacy. With this resource, we want to help you activate what you have already been endowed with, and empower you to fulfill your mandate as an ambassador of blessing to your family.

While the blessing mantle and authority begins with the family, it does not end there. God wants to equip us to be messengers of blessing in enlarged territories—families, communities and other people groups.

> *But I promise you this—the Holy Spirit will come upon you and you will be filled with power. And you will be my messengers to Jerusalem, throughout Judea, the distant provinces—even to the remotest places on earth!* (Acts 1:8 TPT).

What does it look like to be equipped with the mantle of a blessing ambassador?

- The Spirit of the Lord shall rest upon you (Isaiah 11:2; 61:1-4).
- You are sent in the spirit and power of Elijah to realign the hearts of men, women, boys and girls—parents and children—to each other and to the heavenly Father (Malachi 4:5; Luke 1:17).
- Your mouth has been cleansed with a live coal from the altar of God (Isaiah 6:6-7).
- God, the Creator of your mouth, has put His Word in your mouth (Exodus 4:11; Isaiah 51:16; Jeremiah 1:9; Psalm 81:10).
- Like a cargo ship you are packed full of the blessing (Romans 15:29 TPT).

What about your authority?

You saw in Deuteronomy 21:5 that your mandate as a priest is to pronounce blessings in the name of the Lord. Read what Terry and

Melissa Bone have said about this authority:

> *The word "pronounce" carries the connotation of authority. In the same way that a judge's words represent the government that appointed him, so the priests' words of blessing carried the governmental weight of God's authority in the spiritual realm... the authority inherent in a spoken blessing flows from God's partnership with the words. In Hebrew, the phrase translated "pronounce blessings" reads, 'bless by their word and the Lord.' Effectively God was saying: **'If you will speak, I will act.'** God promised to partner with the priests' words to accomplish His spiritual activity in the lives of His people.*[18] (Emphasis is mine).

In the model language that God gave Moses for Aaron and his sons to speak over the Israelites as a blessing, we also see that the Lord's Name is the authority that accomplishes the words of the blessing:

> *And the Lord spoke to Moses, saying: "Speak to Aaron and his sons, saying, 'This is the way you shall bless the children of Israel. Say to them:*
>
> *"The Lord bless you and keep you;*
> *The Lord make His face shine upon you,*
> *And be gracious to you;*
> *The Lord lift up His countenance upon you,*
> *And give you peace."'*
>
> ***"So they shall put My name on the children of Israel, and I will bless them"*** (Numbers 6:22-27, emphasis is mine).

As New Testament priests, we pronounce blessings in the greatest of all names—the Name of Jesus Christ of Nazareth. His Name represents the totality of His person, His finished redemptive work, His authority and His power.

> *He has now been given the greatest of all names! The authority of the name of Jesus causes every knee to bow in reverence! Everything and everyone will one day submit to this name—in the heavenly realm, in the earthly realm, and in the demonic realm* (Philippians 2:9b-10 TPT).

Also, don't forget that because we were created in the image and likeness of God to operate like Him, one dimension of our fundamental birthright is the authority to speak blessings like Him. In addition, as you read earlier, we do have delegated authority from our position of being raised up with Christ and seated with Him in the heavenly realm.

I bless you to be released into your mantle of authority by exercising your faith as you read The Blessing Mantle in Appendix One. Read the words prayerfully and as often as needed until they settle in your spirit and your whole being comes into alignment. You may also find it helpful to change the language to first-person (I and me). The next step is to release The Blessing Mantle over yourself. Or, you may ask your pastor or other spiritual authority to do so. Either way, be blessed into receiving what was yours before the foundation of the earth. I bless you to possess and enjoy your birthright.

Activating Your Mantle

Receiving your mantle is one thing, activating it is another. The first of the priestly mandates identified in Deuteronomy 21:5, is to minister to the Lord, and it is important to keep first things first. I read an article by Dr. Clarice Fluitt which said that the kingdom realm is voice activated.[19] The secret to activating our blessing mantle and authority is to invest time in ministering to the Lord with heartfelt love and adoration.

Sometimes, you may come before the Lord in stillness with a listening heart. As The Passion Translation of Psalm 65:5 says, you may come "…standing in absolute stillness, before the one (you) love." At other times, you will speak words of blessing to Him—eulogizing, praising, and speaking well of Him. King David's poetic praise in the Psalms and other Old Testament books provide us with many examples. I have come to really appreciate the extravagant adoration of 1 Chronicles 29:10-13 (AMPC):

> 10 *Therefore David blessed the Lord before all the assembly and said, Be praised, adored, and thanked, O Lord, the God of Israel our [forefather], forever and ever.*
>
> 11 *Yours, O Lord, is the greatness and the power and the glory and the victory and the majesty, for all that is in the heavens and the earth is Yours; Yours is the kingdom, O Lord, and Yours it is to be exalted as Head over all.*
>
> 12 *Both riches and honor come from You, and You reign over all. In Your hands are power and might; in Your hands it is to make great and to give strength to all.*
>
> 13 *Now therefore, our God, we thank You and praise Your glorious name and those attributes which that name denotes.*

Blessing the Mighty Names of the Lord, as revealed throughout Scripture, is another powerful way to bless the Lord with our words. I found an amazing forty-seven-minute recording by John Paul Jackson on YouTube that is just dripping in the anointing, *I AM. 365 Names of God*[20] When I listen to this recording, it brings me to a deeper place in worshipping and adoring the matchless characteristics, attributes and wonders of God.

When I bless the Lord before speaking a blessing to others, it never fails to unlock the flow of His glorious anointing and authority to and through me. We have the promise of God: "In blessing I will bless you"

(Genesis 22:17a), and He is a faithful Promise Keeper. When you bless the Lord, blessings will flow back and multiply to you and others. The blessings of supernatural wisdom and insight will come to you. You will receive the words to speak in blessing others and you will be empowered to speak them. When you speak the word God gives you, they will be clothed in His power and authority. It will be His words blessing others.

Receive this powerful impartation from the classic devotional, *Come Away My Beloved*, by Frances J. Roberts:

> *You shall be unafraid when you face others, for wisdom is power. You shall be unashamed to speak, for you shall know that the words you speak are not your own, but His who sent you and made you His messenger. You shall be able to testify as did Jesus: "The words that I speak to you I do not speak on My own authority; but the Father who dwells in Me does the works" (John 14:10). Know that I will do it. Trust me to do it. You shall rejoice far in excess of any joy you have yet experienced.*
>
> *Amazing things await you. You have had but the tiniest foretaste. Launch out!*
>
> *I will make you a blessing…I will make you as My ambassador, a sweet savor of life and grace.*[21]

A Blessing From My Heart to Yours

The Lord has blessed me with a good measure of His life-giving words, and I bless you from the overflow of what I have received from Him.

May you be known as someone who gives the gift of life-giving words.

May you be contagiously blessed.

May you be bold, courageous, and faithful to your call, as the One who has called you is faithful.

May you encounter the Father-heart of God and be filled with His matchless love for you.

I bless you from Colossians 3:17—May every activity of your life as a blessing ambassador, and every word that comes from your lips be drenched with the beauty of our Lord Jesus, the Anointed One.

May you bring your constant praise to God the Father for what our Lord Jesus has done for you.

I bless you in the Name of Jesus Christ of Nazareth.

Your

verbal blessings

bring

heaven to earth

and

reconcile

earth to heaven.

Chapter 8

What It Means to Bless

With the insights you have gained about who you are as a blessing ambassador, let's develop a deeper understanding of what it means to bless someone with your gift of words. We will begin with the origin and history of the word "bless," and build on that foundation with an overview of what the spoken blessing accomplishes. This chapter also includes clarification of what the blessing is not, as well as a summary explanation and preamble that may be useful for a blessing ceremony introduction.

Origins of the Word "Bless"

The Hebrew word for "bless" is *barak.* It means to 'bend the knee, to confer a blessing, to praise, to invoke, and to ask or pray a blessing.' The Hebrew custom of a recipient kneeling to receive a blessing reflects this root meaning. But there is something more spectacular about this word. The essence of the words, "The Lord bless you," in the Priestly Blessing is that Father God Himself bends His knees before us to bestow His blessings upon us.[22] How amazing!

The Greek word for "bless" is *eulogeo* from which we get the English word *eulogy*— a word associated with funerals when a chronicle of good things is spoken about the deceased. It means to 'speak well of another, to say good or positive things.' We have mastered the art of eulogizing or speaking well of the dead. How much more we need to build a culture of saying good things to others while they are still alive!

The old Germanic and old English origin of the word "bless" is *blood.*

It means to consecrate or sprinkle with blood.[23] With His blood, Jesus redeemed us out of every curse so that we might receive the blessing. His redemptive work is the source of every blessing (see Ephesians 1:3 and Galatians 3:13-14).

What amazing word pictures and clues to help us understand what God embedded in His design of the spoken blessing!

The Glory of the Blessing

Throughout the Bible, the power of the spoken blessing and what it accomplishes is unveiled before our eyes—from the creation blessings that God spoke in the Book of Genesis to the blessings of adoration poured out on Him in the Book of Revelation. The many stories and testimonies of our time also attest to the supernatural power and glory of verbal blessing.

Everything that God has designed and created has its own glory. Basically, when we speak of the glory of a thing, we mean the expression of its true nature, characteristics and essence. The Hebrew word for "glory" is *kabod*, which carries the idea of 'heavy, weighty, fullness, or full weight.' We can, therefore, say that spoken blessings carry "weight" in the spiritual realm. In one of the testimonials at the end of the book, you will read about someone's revelation of the weightiness of the blessing.

Let's look at some important highlights of what the spoken blessing accomplishes:

- **Affirms** our legitimacy as ones chosen by God to be on the earth at this time, and uniquely designed by Him to serve His purposes in our generation.
- **Builds** supernatural deposits in our heart to heal our past and shape our future.

- **Confers** heaven's favor upon our identity and destiny.
- **Conveys** to us a sense of belonging, love, honor, dignity, value, worth and significance.
- **Covers** us with the New Covenant blood of Jesus by which we were redeemed from the curse to receive the blessing.
- **Empowers** us to prosper.
- **Imparts** the supernatural power of God into our lives.
- **Infuses** God's divine provision into all that concerns us.
- **Invokes** God's presence in our lives.
- **Places** the Name of God upon us for us to experience His glorious person, character and attributes.

Ephesians 1:17 describes the heavenly Father as the "Father of glory." Intentional words spoken on His behalf have the authority and power to accomplish all of this and more. How stupendous! The spoken blessing is indeed a treasure chest of extravagant riches from our heavenly Father!

Border Crossings and Questions

According to Terry and Melissa Bone, our seven major life stages are like border crossings, with a unique life question associated with each one. In the context of these border crossings and our journey from one to the next, the blessing accomplishes something marvelous—it empowers us to have a safe and fulfilling journey through the pivotal stages of life.

When we travel from Canada to the United States, for example, U.S. border security requires that we answer at least two basic questions: "Where are you going?" and "Why?" If we are unable to answer these questions, we are either detained or turned back. Conversely, if we answer the questions, we receive clearance to proceed. Similarly, our crossing from one life-stage to the next requires that we answer certain questions. When we receive verbal blessings on a regular basis as a normal part of our upbringing, we are empowered to confidently answer the major life question related to each stage of our development (see Appendix Two).

In many instances, our lives tell the story of the consequences of missed family blessings: arrested development and misdirected energy to compensate for insecurities, fear and unmet needs. However, it's not too late to turn things around.

It's time to recover your missed blessings and break the cycle for future generations. I believe you are reading this book because you are part of God's master plan for the building of a culture of verbal blessing to transform lives and our culture. As a blessing ambassador, you will be fulfilling the eternal plan of God for you that Ephesians 2:10 describes. Let me personalize the last part of the verse from The Passion Translation—"Even before [you] were born, God planned in advance [your] destiny and the good works you would do to fulfill it!"

My prayer is that this resource will be a helpful tool in your hands.

I want to move on now to some important points of clarification to bear in mind.

A Blessing is Not a Prayer

Prayer brings earth's petitions to heaven, while blessing brings heaven's provision to earth. This is the clearest way I have been able to distinguish between the two. We are so familiar with prayer that it is often assumed that a blessing and a prayer are one and the same, but they are not.

Blessings
turbo-charge
us with divine
empowerment!

Remember Ephesians 1:3—"Blessed be the God and Father of our Lord Jesus Christ, who has blessed us with every spiritual blessing in the heavenly places in Christ." Intentionally spoken words on behalf of God the Father are the primary vehicle for bringing spiritual blessings from the heavenly realm to the spirit and heart of a person.

Although a blessing is different from a prayer, it is important to know that they are not entirely independent of each other. You will find these extracts from Terry and Melissa Bone's book very helpful in understanding the role of prayer:

> *Prayer ought to accompany a blessing, but it does not replace it. People who do not understand this will often revert to praying when asked to participate in a blessing ceremony. Typically, they bow their heads, close their eyes and ask God to bless the person for whom they are praying. However, asking God to bless someone is not the same as giving them a blessing yourself! A blessing should be spoken in the first person using direct eye contact. Prayer may then play a role as part of the active commitment that follows.*[24]

Since the spoken blessing is designed to transform lives with freedom, healing and restoration, as a result, it often comes up against strong resistance. Therefore, prayer is a very necessary follow-through:

> *The forces of Satan and the weakness in our human nature constantly conspire to war against our spiritual growth and advancement. In times of war, every breakthrough requires a follow-through. The delivery of a spoken blessing can represent a powerful breakthrough in a person's life. Without appropriate follow-through, however, the value of a blessing can be robbed from a person's future experience.* [25]

Using the analogy of seeds, I think of spoken blessings as "word seeds" planted in a person's heart—they must be watered to bear fruit. Prayer is to the blessing what water is to freshly sown seeds. The bottom line is that we need to do both—bless and pray!

Five Other Things That the Spoken Blessing is Not

1. **The blessing is not merely positive speaking.** The blessing far surpasses positive speaking because when we speak words of blessing, we are engaged in the transmission of divine power, authority, and much more.

2. **The blessing is not merely verbal affirmation.** The practice of speaking personal affirmations is widely embraced as a means of building one's confidence and self-esteem. While affirmations have great value, they lack the authority and power inherent in words of blessing.

3. **The blessing is not merely words of encouragement.** Words of encouragement are like the uplifting breath of fresh air we all need. Verbal blessings come with plenty of encouragement and a whole lot more. Blessings turbo-charge us with divine empowerment!

4. **The blessing is not merely a heartfelt wish.** While good wishes from others are uplifting, they cannot do for us what an impartation from heaven accomplishes. Verbal blessings are impartations from heaven.

5. **A blessing is not a prophecy.** I am going to elaborate on this point to ensure that no one disqualifies himself or herself, because of the misconception that speaking a blessing involves giving someone a "prophetic word."

   A verbal blessing is not the same as giving a specific word of prophecy about a person's future. However, one element of the family blessing (especially when children are being

> blessed by parents and grandparents) does involve discerning and speaking into the special future God has designed for them. The blessing carries the authority to help shape a person's identity and destiny according to their God-given purpose. It is in this context that I previously referred to the spoken blessing as a prophetic instrument for shaping lives and destiny.

When Introducing the Blessing to Others

The spoken blessing is a relatively new phenomenon to most individuals, so it may need a bit of an introduction. Whenever I have a gathering of individuals attending a blessing ceremony, I find it extremely beneficial to begin with a few words about what the blessing is and what it accomplishes. The preamble usually raises the level of interest and expectation.

I often begin with a summary explanation that goes something like this:

> There are different kinds of blessing mentioned in the Bible. The blessing we are here to impart is the kind that God established at creation when He blessed all humanity in Adam. We are talking about verbal blessing which, in a nutshell, is the speaking of intentional words on behalf of God the Father, in His authority, and by the power of the Holy Spirit.
>
> God intended spoken blessings to be the birthright gift to each person—just for being born. He also intended that these blessings would be deposited into a person's heart at pivotal stages of development. Most of us missed them. But there's good news—it's never too late to catch up because of the complete redemptive work that Jesus accomplished on our behalf.

I may also incorporate a quick overview of some or all of the following points in the preamble, depending on the occasion:

- What intentionally spoken words of blessing accomplish.
- The importance of blessing in the Jewish culture as a normal way of life and as the most coveted thing.
- The seven life stages of development and related questions.
- The fact that our human spirit is not limited by time and space so we can go back and recover the blessings that we were meant to receive from the time of our conception to the present.
- A reference to Galatians 3:13-14 and Ephesians 1:3 to highlight the redemptive work of Jesus that now makes it possible for us to receive our missed blessings.

Let me reiterate how our lives are affected by the absence or presence of spoken blessings, especially pivotal life-stage blessings: "When we possess them in abundance, we prosper in life without striving. When they are absent, we struggle in life in spite of our valiant efforts."[26]

There's great news! Your blessings are waiting for you and you need not live without them. Others around you need not live without them either. I sense a wave of hope arising!

May God make you His messenger of hope and an effective channel of spoken blessings to many. May you be contagiously blessed!

Chapter 9

Blessing Essentials

A wave of hope ushered us out of the last chapter, and now we can move into the practical aspect of giving a blessing to someone. There's plenty of help available to you!

Your main go-to source for the nuts and bolts of giving a verbal blessing is the book by Terry and Melissa Bone: *The Family Blessing Guidebook: Everything You Need to Know to Have a Blessed Family.* Their book includes many sample blessings as well as a very useful format for crafting blessings. Appendix Four provides a list that will give you an idea of what is available to you. You may purchase *The Family Blessing Guidebook* online at www.powerofblessing.com.

Although verbal blessings are spirit driven, not formula driven, the sample blessings and guidelines from *The Family Blessing Guidebook* have been quite helpful to me. They were my training wheels at the outset until gradually, with the help of the Holy Spirit, I started adding my unique "flavor" to the blessings that I crafted and spoke. I am so very grateful for my early beginnings.

As you would have read in the preface, the assignment the Lord gave me for this manual is to synergize and supplement, not reinvent. You will see from the bibliography that I had the privilege of drawing from several sources as a foundation. With insights from these sources, the Scriptures, and what the Holy Spirit has taught me over these thirteen-plus years, here is a consolidated list of various essentials that will give you a jumpstart and sustain you in fulfilling your mantle as a blessing ambassador:

1. First things first.
2. Start where you are.
3. Pray.
4. Develop a hearing heart.
5. Learn and practice the language of blessing.
6. Bless spirit-to-spirit.
7. Exercise your authority.
8. Bless by faith.

1. First things first

I learned the phrase "first things first" in the 1990s when reading the book by Stephen Covey, *The 7 Habits of Highly Effective People.*[27] The idea behind this principle is to give priority to tasks that contribute the most to our effectiveness as people of purpose with strong values. When it comes to the spiritual matter of building a legacy of blessing, the recovery of your missed blessing is a high priority.

It is truly more blessed to give than to receive (Acts 20:35). However, we cannot give what we have not received. Receiving the life-stage blessings that you missed is therefore the first step in becoming equipped as a blessing ambassador. I shared my story earlier and you can be sure that what the heavenly Father did for me, He will also do for you.

In catching up on your missed life-stage blessings, the most essential thing is to encounter the Father-heart of God and to receive His matchless love for you. The blessing that God spoke to Adam did not only convey identity, destiny, and authority, it flowed from God's Father-heart of love for Adam as a son (see Luke 3:38). As a blessing ambassador, you should seek above all things to know this Father-heart of God for yourself—by personal experience. The heavenly Father's love is the ultimate fulfillment that each person seeks. When the blessing flows from your love-filled heart, others will encounter the Father's love through you.

The Blessing Recovery Clinic in Part Two is dedicated to facilitating your journey of recovery. You may give a parent, spouse, spiritual authority or other mature believer in Christ the access and permission to deposit these blessing treasures into your heart. Or you may take the route that I took, which was to fasten my faith to each word of blessing I read and open my heart to receive the deposit. Either way, it is the Holy Spirit who pours out the love of God into our hearts (see Romans 5:5). He administers the deposit.

2. Start where you are

This is my foremost encouragement to you, so I am going to say it again, this time in capital letters: START WHERE YOU ARE! As I shared earlier, I am glad I did not hold back from speaking blessings to others. I have adopted this statement as one of my blessing mottos: "Even a poorly delivered blessing is much better than no blessing at all."[28]

Drawing on my own experience, I have a few guiding thoughts to share with you:

- **Start with yourself.** Speak the life-stage blessings over yourself and get into the practice of daily engaging your spirit with words of blessing.
- **You have everything you need.** God designed and wired you for

verbal blessings—to receive and speak them. The Holy Spirit, who dwells in you through faith in Jesus, is your empowerment. Trust Him to guide you and release divine power through the words you speak.

- **Begin with small steps.** You may be familiar with this ancient Chinese proverb: "A journey of a thousand miles begins with a single step." Verbal blessing is a new art, language and culture that you are beginning to assimilate. Although you have the capacity for blessing in your spiritual DNA, as with most things, there is a necessary process to mature into that capacity. Here's a tip for your debut: write out the blessing you plan to speak and read it to the recipient. It doesn't mean you won't do that later as well, for as I shared earlier, that was the instruction from the Holy Spirit which led to the birth of the Blessing Recovery Clinic.

- **Push through feelings of insecurity or fear.** You may be worried about not sounding eloquent or afraid that you will make mistakes. What matters in the end, however, is not how articulate or impressive we are. It is reassuring to know that even the Apostle Paul dealt with insecurity and fear. He said to the Corinthians: "When I came to you, I did not come with eloquence or human wisdom…I came to you in weakness with great fear and trembling. My message and my preaching were not with wise and persuasive words, but with a **demonstration of the Spirit's power,** so that your faith might not rest on human wisdom, but on God's power" (1 Corinthians 2:1, 3-5 NIV, emphasis is mine). That's what we're after—a demonstration of the Spirit's power!

- **Be yourself.** I learned a long time ago from the late Dr. Myles Munroe, that I did not want to be a counterfeit when I could be an exquisite original. Create your own flavor of spoken blessings and deliver them in the unique way that reflects your one-of-a-kind divine design. When introduced to the teachings of Terry and Melissa Bone, I knew from the very beginning that God had given me a unique flavor with a strong remedial focus. So after you have gone through the Blessing Recovery Clinic, I release you to make it uniquely yours so that whenever you impart the life-stage blessings to others, it flows from **your** heart.

3. Pray

Remember, prayer is not the same as blessing. However, prayer is a necessary accompaniment that enhances the overall effectiveness of a blessing. Pray for divine wisdom and understanding as you become established as a blessing ambassador. Pray for spiritual discernment as you prepare for blessing opportunities. Prior to a blessing ceremony, prepare the spiritual atmosphere through prayer. Also pray for the recipient and others to have an engaged spirit and open heart. Even while speaking a blessing, pray inwardly and be sensitive to any new insights or words the Holy Spirit may give you. Finally, water the seeds of blessing with prayer, and encourage the recipient and others to do the same. Prayer is an essential follow-through.

4. Develop a hearing heart

Having spiritual discernment and being sensitive to the leading of the Holy Spirit are vital. These qualities come from a hearing heart. Many individuals think that they are unable to hear God, but that is not the truth. We are wired to hear God and may just need to tune into His frequency through our human spirit. If this is an area of challenge, I encourage you to practice having quiet times in the presence of the Lord and bless your spirit with the activation and enlarging of its capacity to hear from God.

Why is it so important to have a hearing heart? A blessing is most effective when it speaks to the unique needs or specific characteristics

Push through

feelings of insecurity or fear.

Be Yourself!

of a person. You may know certain things in the natural about the blessing recipient. With insights from the Holy Spirit, however, your blessing will be a whole lot more powerful. Insights about the person's potential and unique design, the specific Scriptures to use, the crafting of the words of blessing, and how to creatively deliver the blessing are some of the areas where you will need to hear from the Holy Spirit.

Isaiah 50:4, is a verse I often declare over myself: "The Lord God has given me the tongue of the learned, that I should know how to speak a word in season to him who is weary. He awakens me morning by morning, He awakens my ear to hear as the learned." I encourage you to pronounce this verse as a blessing or declaration over yourself as well as ask God for "an understanding mind and a hearing heart," as Solomon did (1 Kings 3:9 AMPC).

5. Learn and practice the language of blessing

Of all His wonderful creatures, humans are the only ones with whom God shared His ability to speak words. Language shapes and represents a culture in the natural and in the spiritual realm. The culture and language of blessing are unique. It will therefore take time, intentional effort and practice to learn that language.

The core component of a verbal blessing are words, and God's Word is the number one source for the words you need to craft a blessing. While all words are powerful, the Word of God is in a league of its own, surpassing all others. God's Word conveys His life, love, wisdom, authority, power, and presence and so much more. This is what Hebrews 4:12 tells us about the Word of God: "For the word of God is living and powerful, and sharper than any two-edged sword, piercing even to the division of soul and spirit, and of joints and marrow, and is a discerner of the thoughts and intents of the heart." Equally important, God's Word is always profitable because He watches over His Word until it is fulfilled (see Jeremiah 1:12; Isaiah 55:10-11).

How do you know which Scriptures to use in crafting a blessing? Based on the person, needs, circumstances and occasion, the Holy Spirit will help you to discern the focus for each blessing and related Scriptures. You can also use Bible Gateway, Google, or other tools to search for Scriptures. Most verses can be easily adapted into a blessing with two simple words added at the beginning: "*May God...*" Or, you may take the central idea of a verse and craft a blessing around it. *The Power of Spoken Blessings* by Bill Gothard[29] is an excellent resource for developing this skill. Appendix Six also provides two lists to help you get started.

You may already be accustomed to praying the Word of God to increase your prayer power. You can integrate that same power into the blessings you craft.

6. Bless Spirit-to-Spirit

The spoken blessing is a spiritual phenomenon and is most effective when it is imparted from your spirit to the spirit of the recipient, not at the intellectual level or soul-to-soul. While you are learning the nuts and bolts of crafting a blessing, you will also want to be intentional about engaging, validating and nurturing your own spirit.

A large part of the process of becoming equipped as a blessing ambassador takes place in the realm of your soul. However, your spirit already knows everything you are trying to learn. You will notice remarkable increase in wisdom and discernment when you feed and nurture your spirit with the Word of God. You can unlock the potential in your spirit by blessing it with words that acknowledge how God designed it to function. In addition, encourage your soul to bless the Lord, as King David did in Psalm 103:1-2, and to cooperate with God's design for your soul to be led by your spirit.

You may engage the spirit of the recipient (including babies in the womb) by inviting them to listen with their spirit. We use this language frequently in the Blessing Recovery Clinic because it is only by our spirit (which knows no boundary of time or space) that we can go back in time and receive the deposits of missed blessing.

7. Exercise your authority

This element of exercising your authority involves above all, a consciousness that you are seated with Christ in the heavenly realm (see Ephesians 2:6). As stated earlier, you are a bi-locational being. Having a consciousness of your position in Christ will activate your blessing mantle of authority.

The authority that backs your words of blessing is in the Name of Jesus. He has been given the greatest of all names and exalted to the place of supreme authority in the heavenly realm (see Philippians 2:9-10; Ephesians 1:20-21). We also gather from the Priestly Blessing in Numbers 6:22-27 that God's Name is the authority behind the words of the spoken blessing. Verse 27 states: "So they shall put my name on the Children of Israel and I will bless them."

I encourage you to familiarize yourself with the many Names by which God has revealed Himself in Scripture. Blessings that invoke a specific Name of God impart deposits of the character, attributes and provision associated with that Name into the spirit and heart of the recipient. Arthur Burk's book, *Blessing Your Spirit*, includes a twenty-one-day treasure chest of blessing your spirit with the Names of God. You will find a sample in Appendix Five.

8. Bless by faith

Your faith is the key that unlocks, releases, and transfers the blessings stored up in the heavenly realm to the heart of the person being blessed. This faith component is highlighted in Hebrews 11:20-21: "By faith Isaac blessed Jacob and Esau concerning things to come. By faith Jacob, when he was dying, blessed each of the sons of Joseph, and worshiped, leaning on the top of his staff."

It is important that you speak blessings from a sincere heart of love and from a posture of faith, because others have a way of detecting whether or not your words convey love and faith. When your faith is locked into the blessing you are imparting, it acts as a catalyst to activate the recipient's faith.

Have faith in God—in his Father-heart of love which longs for His children to receive His blessings, and in His authority and power to bring forth good fruit from the words of blessing you speak. Here is a promise on which you can fasten your faith: "So those who rely on faith are blessed along with Abraham, the man of faith" (Galatians 3:9 NIV).

The Important Element of Touch

From the Scriptures, traditions in the Jewish culture, and the Christian ceremony of dedicating children to the Lord, we see that a meaningful touch is an important component of the blessing.

- Isaac was blind and laid in bed at the time of his blessing impartation, but the element of touch was not missed since Jacob "came near and kissed him" (see Genesis 27:27).

- Jacob embraced his grandsons and laid his hands on their head (see Genesis 48:10, 13-16).

- Simeon embraced baby Jesus in blessing Him and His parents when they came into the temple (see Luke 2:28).

- Jesus took the little children in His arms, laid hands on them and blessed them (see Mark 10:16).

Whether it is a warm embrace, the laying on of hands, a touch, or a handshake, these actions amount to an impartation that conveys something significant to the blessing recipient—love, favor, sincerity, value, empowerment, and more. We cannot underestimate the power of a touch. In the Gospel, we see the manifestation of miracles whenever Jesus touched someone, including a leper being healed and cleansed (see Matthew 8:3, 9:29; Luke 7:14, 22:51).

A Three-fold Cord

In summary, the many different elements of the blessing amount to weaving a three-fold cord:

> *Words say it! Deeds show it! Ceremonies seal it!...Deeds make words more acceptable...add weight and credibility to what we say...Ceremonies validate memorable moments of blessings in our lives with actions that reinforce the sincerity of the words spoken.* [30]

I will never forget the response from a teenager who was on a path of rebellion when her mother surprised her with a birthday blessing ceremony. With hands grasping her chest and with tear-filled eyes, she exclaimed: "*You did this for ME?*" The power of the blessing eclipsed the rebellion in her heart and launched her on God's path to a new beginning.

As Ecclesiastes 4:12 says, "...a three-fold cord is not quickly broken." In the next chapter, you will see that we have countless opportunities to weave these three-fold cords of transformation.

Chapter 10

Blessing Opportunities

Imagine a cargo ship loaded with treasures . . .

Let me put this image into perspective by sharing with you Romans 15:29 from The Passion Translation: "I am convinced that when I come to you, I will come packed full and loaded with the blessings of the Anointed One!" The footnote to this verse tells us that the word for "loaded" in Greek is *pleroma*, and that this word is "…also used for a cargo ship packed full of people and goods."

How would you like to be known as a person who is like a cargo ship loaded with treasures of transformation—*packed full and loaded with blessings*?

Can you see how much it would delight the heart of the heavenly Father that His sons and daughters are filling the earth with His glory? "For the earth will be filled with the knowledge of the glory of the Lord, as the waters cover the sea" (Habakkuk 2:14).

God's intent was for Adam and Eve to take the divine design and glory of the Garden of Eden to the rest of the created earth, but they fell into sin before fulfilling their mission. We have redemption through Jesus Christ, however, and our dominion mandate and privilege to fill the earth with the glory of God have been redeemed. We have been restored so that we can fulfill our mandate of blessing creation with a foretaste of its anticipated freedom (see Romans 8:19-23). Remember, God has given us the authority to bless people, places, and things.

The possibilities are endless!

The more you embrace your mantle as an ambassador of blessing, the more conscious you will become of the many opportunities around you. Hardly a day will pass without you speaking words of blessing. It may be a simple "God bless you" said with more meaning than before, since you now have a greater consciousness of the authority and power behind those words. Before long, you will find spontaneous words of blessings flowing from your heart to the hearts of people, over places, and over things. Fill your heart with love for God and people, with the Word of God, with faith, and with a passion for kingdom transformation. When you do this, you will surely experience the blessing overflow. It's a biblical principle: "A good man out of the good treasure of his heart brings forth good…For out of the abundance of the heart his mouth speaks" (Luke 6:45).

Reflecting on the creation model, you will recall that God spoke three kinds of blessings at creation. The first related to identity and destiny; the second to authority and provision; and the third to time.[31] We could call this a "blessing operations blueprint." In one way or another, the opportunities available to us fall within the scope of this blueprint.

Now, let's zoom in a bit and unpack some of those opportunities.

Who to Bless

Anyone and everyone! The Holy Spirit gave me a wide-open playing field very early on by impressing two things on my heart: It isn't always necessary to know the person for whom a blessing is intended, and the blessing doesn't always have to be spoken directly to that person. The blessing simply had to be released in faith. During that time, expectant mothers seemed to pop up all around me, especially on the subway to and from work. On a few occasions, I even had strong impressions to send a blessing to women who didn't appear to be pregnant and I was also supplied with words to bless either their new pregnancy or their womb for conception. I also remember feeling really awkward one day, only to receive a reassurance in my spirit: *Eternity will tell.*

I am thankful for God's grace that enabled me to walk in obedience on those occasions when I felt silly about speaking into the atmosphere. I later realized that these were bona fide blessings because there are no limits to the Spirit-life of faith-filled words. I was also in training and didn't know it, for many women have since given me the privilege of blessing their womb prior to conception and during pregnancy.

I have adopted a prayer motto from Philippians 4:6, and Armin Gesswein, a leader who influenced the prayer movement in the United States in the twentieth century: "Prayer is not everything but everything is by prayer." In addition, I also have a blessing motto: "Everyone needs a blessing and I have one to give." Whether it is someone on the street or in the news, I seize the moments as they come. May your spirit be sensitive to the Holy Spirit and recognize your moments of opportunity. May you also seize each opportunity, even if it feels or sounds awkward.

The following list is far from complete and is intended to serve as a catalyst to bring to mind opportunities that you may not have thought of:

- Bless the Lord (His Name, attributes, etc.).
- Bless yourself.
- Bless your spouse (including your future spouse if you are not yet married).
- Bless your children and grandchildren (including their friends and future spouse).
- Bless your parents and grandparents (although they may not have

known how to bless you).

- Bless your in-laws.
- Bless your extended family.
- Bless your generational line.
- Bless your church family (including pastors and leaders).
- Bless your government officials.
- Bless your employer, doctor, and other service providers.
- Bless your neighbours.
- Bless your friends.
- Bless your enemies (as Luke 6:28 and Romans 12:20 instruct us to do).
- Bless the next generation of parents, politicians, kingdom and marketplace leaders.
- Bless the youth and young adults.
- Bless the prodigals.
- Bless single parent families.
- Bless mothers and fathers.
- Bless newlyweds.
- Bless new parents.
- Bless new teens (with a Rites of Passage ceremony).[32]

In September 2017, I had the privilege of imparting a blessing to thirty-nine newly inducted chaplains. In that ceremony, as instructed by the Holy Spirit, I formally released the blessing mantle for the first time.[33] A few weeks later, the Lord spoke to me concerning unique niches that were available to these chaplains, who in His eyes were set apart as blessing ambassadors. They had countless opportunities to adopt spheres of influence in the spirit and regularly pronounce blessings over their adopted sphere(s) and the people within them. It would be somewhat like the "virtual blessing" ministry the Lord had given me for expectant mothers.

For example, they could:

- Bless men and boys to strengthen fatherhood in our culture.
- Bless nursing home seniors with honor, inner harmony, and freedom in Christ.
- Bless youth in trouble with the law to have new beginnings.
- Bless individuals with mental health challenges.

So can you as a blessing ambassador!

WHAT to Bless

Transforming lives and culture with the gift of words is our overarching mission as blessing ambassadors. This means that our two primary targets are people and cultural spheres.

Blessing people. When it comes to blessing people, the blessing of each major life stage, or the "family blessing," is the fundamental birthright of every person, and no one should have to live without these blessings. You will have opportunity to give these blessings to individuals of all ages who need to recover what they missed. As blessing ambassadors, we are also committed to turning things around for generations to come by mentoring future parents and grandparents to be proactive in giving the gift of spoken blessings on a regular basis to their children and grandchildren.

In addition to the fundamental life-stage blessings, we have the opportunity to speak blessings at other major milestones in a person's life. Blessing someone's name is an excellent way to speak blessing into their life because of how much names reflect one's identity and destiny. There are many online sources for finding the meanings of a name. *The Name Book* by Dorothy Astoria is a great resource as it gives both the inherent meaning and the spiritual connotation of each name, as well as a Scripture verse.[34] You will find a sample name blessing in Appendix Seven.

Since discovering the two books by Arthur Burk: *Blessing Your Spirit* and *Blessing your Soul,* I have now also enlarged my scope to include the blessing of a person's spirit and soul. This is a relatively new territory that you may want to explore. I have included a sample from each book in Appendix Five. The books are also available from his website at www.theslg.com.

Blessing culture. The concept of the "Seven Cultural Mountains" [35] or cultural spheres emerged in the 1970s, and help us to identify the major areas that influence society and shape the way we think:

- Religion
- Family
- Education
- Government
- Media
- Arts and entertainment
- Business

The heart of God is that His kingdom culture would invade these "Mountains." Everyone does not have spiritual jurisdictional authority over these areas. However, with the authority of our blessing mantle, we can invade these areas with spoken blessings. These are significant areas of deployment for us as blessing ambassadors, so I encourage you to seek guidance from the Lord as to which area(s) He would have you adopt. A ministry called *The House of Good Hope* provides a prayer guide with Scriptures for praying through each "Mountain."[36] As mentioned before, many Scriptures used for prayer can be easily turned into a verbal blessing.

WHEN to Bless

The Apostle Paul admonished us to "Pray without ceasing" (1 Thessalonians 5:17). The same holds true for the blessing: Bless without ceasing!

Ultimately, we want to see spoken blessings become a way of life—a normal part of everyday life—because that is what God intended from the beginning. The Jewish people have mastered this way of life. We can learn from the pros. We shared in Chapter Six how Jacob was instrumental in establishing a legacy of blessing. His legacy has been sustained from generation to generation through weekly Shabbat family blessings and through spontaneous day-to-day verbal blessings. Aaron Früh gives us a sense of how normal verbal blessings were used in ancient Jewish culture; "Speaking a blessing was as natural for Jacob as shaking hands is to us."[37] The Book of Ruth is an excellent example with at least eight spoken blessings in just four short chapters.

In seeking to restore the culture of blessing, we want to be intentional about this combination of formal ceremonies and spontaneous everyday blessings. Andrea Boweya is the author of *Legacy Moments*, a creative keepsake book for transferring intangible generational wealth and other legacy treasures to the next generation. Her encouragement is to "Make every moment a Legacy Moment."

Melissa Bone puts it this way: "Use any event as an opportunity to bless."

Although Deuteronomy 6:6-7 does not use the word "bless," it certainly endorses the principle of spontaneous blessings:

> *And these words that I command you today shall be on your heart. You shall teach them diligently to your children, and shall talk of them when you sit in your house, and when you walk by the way, and when you lie down, and when you rise.*

While we are on the way to where we need to be, it may be beneficial for families with children to set apart intentional family times of blessing. It's easy for busy schedules to get in the way, so the commitment to a set time will help to establish the blessing as a normal part of the family lifestyle. Make these times enjoyable and uplifting so that everyone looks forward to them. Be creative and willing to make changes as you figure out what works best for your family.[38]

Two Model Blessings for Creating Your Own Spiritual Heritage

The ancient Jewish patriarch, Jacob, established the legacy of verbal blessing. For generations, Jewish families have enlarged the heritage. Why not create your own spiritual heritage of blessing that will outlive you and enrich generations to come?

God has provided us with two model or staple blessings, and we will have endless opportunities to speak them. They can be used as stand-alone blessings or incorporated into a crafted blessing. Both are suitable for formal ceremonies and for day-to-day use. The Jewish people include both in their Shabbat blessing.

1. The Ephraim and Manasseh Blessing of Genesis 48:20

"So he blessed them that day, saying,
By you Israel will bless, saying,
'May God make you as Ephraim and as Manasseh!'"

I had the privilege of giving the Ephraim and Manasseh blessing to two of my fellow intercessors. They were familiar with the Scripture verse. However, they received new revelation when I extended the blessing to reflect the meanings of the names:
Manasseh— "making forgetful"
Ephraim— "fruitfulness."

"May God make you like Ephraim and Manasseh—may He cause you to **forget the pain of your past**, including the pain of your father's house, and may He make you **fruitful and prosperous in the future**."

They were both deeply impacted. They called this Ephraim and Manasseh blessing the "core blessing" that every person should receive repeatedly throughout his or her life. A few days earlier, my husband had also spoken this same blessing to one of our sons on his birthday. It was his greatest birthday gift.

Who doesn't have something painful from the past to forget and who doesn't want to be fruitful in the future? This is indeed reminiscent of what God said through the prophet Isaiah: "Forget the former things; do not dwell on the past. See, I am doing a new thing!" (Isaiah 43:18-19a).

Memorize and meditate on this short but potent blessing so that you have it ready in your spirit when an opportunity arises. I believe the blessing is just as powerful if the names Ephraim and Manasseh are not included, especially when the recipient is a female or someone who does not have much of a biblical background.

2. The Priestly Blessing of Numbers 6:24-27

24 *"The Lord bless you and keep you;*
25 *The Lord make His face shine upon you,*
And be gracious to you;
26 *The Lord lift up His countenance upon you,*
And give you peace.'"
27 *"So they shall put My name on the children of Israel, and I will bless them."*

You will have many opportunities to pronounce this blessing within your family circle and beyond. When you bless someone with this Priestly Blessing (also known as the Aaronic blessing), know that with each of these God-breathed words, you are putting the Name of Father God on the recipient—His person, character, authority, and supernatural powers. You are giving God a voice when you pronounce this blessing.

Speak the Priestly blessing over yourself, memorize it and meditate on it until it gets into your spirit and becomes a natural part of you. This was the staple blessing that I gave to my daughter each morning as she left to attend classes at the university. One morning she was in a hurry and left without it. She returned that evening and announced that leaving home without the blessing made her realize the difference it had been making each day.

Sometimes the Priestly Blessing is described as a "Prayer of Blessing." However, we don't need to get hung up on the terminology. Although Numbers 6:24-26 is normally used as a blessing, it can be adapted as a powerful prayer. *The Amplified Hebrew to English Interpretation,* by Warren M. Marcus, supplies language that is very useful for intercession. Appendix Three includes this special interpretation.

Be free in your spirit and follow the guidance of the Holy Spirit on how to use this model blessing in any given situation. Remember the key: just as many Scripture passages can be adapted and used as a blessing, this blessing can also be adapted as a prayer. In the case of Numbers 6:24-26, we are talking about not only God-breathed words, but God-prescribed words! When we pray these words back to God, they go up to Him as "highest praise"—the kind that executes vengeance on the enemy (see Psalm 149:6-9 and the testimonial on the revelation received in a dream about the "weight" of the blessing).

These two model blessings are precious treasures with which we can all load our cargo ships. They also provide practical opportunities for learning and practicing the language of blessing which we mentioned in the previous chapter.

Congratulations! You have been diligent in making it through to this point, and now you are only one chapter away from the Blessing Recovery Clinic in Part Two. We do not want anything to impede the flow of your heavenly Father's blessing to your heart or the fruit it will bear in your life, so let's take the opportunity in the next chapter to identify and remove any potential blockers.

Bless without Ceasing.

Chapter 11

Blessing Blockers

It has been a long time coming. Finally, you've identified that missing "something" you've been waiting for—your birthright of spoken family blessings that you did not receive. Your days of waiting are over. Your best and most blessed days are here! It's recovery time. What can stop you now? A few things could, potentially. However, with the passionate determination you've shown to get to this point, I know that you will let nothing stand between you and these treasures.

Let's pray:

Holy Spirit, you are a revealer of the deep secrets of the heart, so we invite you now to unveil every potential blocker and supply the grace needed to overcome. We ask this in the authority of the mighty Name of Jesus Christ of Nazareth. Amen.

May I encourage you to also say this prayer out loud, asking the Holy Spirit to locate any blockages:

> *God, I invite your searching gaze into my heart.*
> *Examine me through and through;*
> *find out everything that may be hidden within me.*
> *Put me to the test and sift through all my anxious cares.*
> *See if there is any path of pain I'm walking on,*
> *and lead me back to your glorious, everlasting ways—*
> *the path that brings me back to you* (Psalm 139:23-24 TPT).
>
> *Amen.*

Some Potential Blockers

We are not engaging in an exercise of personal introspection. The Holy Spirit is the One who must do the work. He is aware of what is buried in the subconscious, and He supplies the necessary grace. Allow Him to walk you through this list of potential blockers and help you to identify any that are relevant to you, as well as anything else that may not be on the list.

- Inability to receive the heavenly Father's love
- Imposing images of imperfect earthly fathers onto the heavenly Father
- Doubting God and His Word
- Idolatry—giving first place to something or someone other than God
- Unwillingness to grant forgiveness to others, yourself, and even God, for past trauma
- Believing that the pain of the past is too deep to be healed
- Believing lies that past experiences have told you about yourself
- Self-condemnation
- Self-hatred
- Self-protection
- Fear of letting go
- Difficulty trusting anyone
- Thinking it is too late
- Pride

- An unbelieving heart
- A closed heart
- Strongholds of sinful habits
- Having an untamed tongue accustomed to speaking curses
- Strongholds of generational or personal involvement in occult practices
- ______________________________
- ______________________________
- ______________________________

Prayer of Repentance and Deliverance

Now, once again, I invite you to audibly pray from a sincere heart this prayer of repentance and deliverance:

> Heavenly Father, I bring before you each blockage that the spotlight of your Holy Spirit has located in me. I confess them before you as sin and repent of them. I ask you, Heavenly Father, to fill me with your Spirit of grace, and accomplish in me what I cannot do for myself or on my own strength.
>
> Through the blood of Jesus, I renounce every identified blockage and ask your forgiveness for having allowed them to form. I give you permission, Father, to root out each one, and to destroy every stronghold by your mighty power. Where I previously withheld forgiveness from others, myself, or even you, God, I now grant that forgiveness from my heart in the Name of Jesus.

> I pray as Jesus taught us to pray: forgive me the wrongs I have done as I release forgiveness to those who have wronged me (or I thought had wronged me). I ask you to continue to cleanse me from all unrighteousness. Create in me a clean heart, I ask, and renew a right spirit in me. Let the words of my mouth and the meditation of my heart be acceptable in Your sight, O Lord, my strength and my Redeemer. Thank you for leading me back to your glorious, everlasting ways—the path that brings me back to you.[39] In the mighty Name of Jesus Christ of Nazareth I pray. Amen.

According to John 8:36, I proclaim over you that Jesus Christ, the Son, sets you free and you are free indeed!

Praying for the Heart Condition of Blessing Recipients

Once you have recovered your missed blessings, you will be well on your way to helping others do the same. It is also important to take the time to help your recipients remove any blockers that may obstruct the flow of their blessing. How you go about doing that will depend on the person and the situation. Be aware, however, that you can always pray for their spiritual heart and ask the Holy Spirit to do a thorough reconditioning of the soil of their heart for the blessing to be fruitful in their lives.

Why is the condition of the spirit and heart so important? God designed spoken blessings to be received by our human spirit, deposited into the heart, and transmitted to the soul and body. The condition of the spirit and heart of the recipient contributes to the effectiveness of a verbal blessing—how much of it gets into the heart and how much fruit it bears.

The

Holy Spirit

supplies the necessary

Grace.

The parable of the sower in Matthew 13 gives us a good sense of how the heart condition determines what can happen to the spoken blessing we give to others:

- **Closed heart:** The blessing falls by the wayside and is devoured. As powerful as words of blessing are, if they don't land in the heart, they won't accomplish what they are sent to do. The deposit of the blessing in the heart will be intercepted. You may encounter closed heart situations when someone invites you to do a blessing on behalf of others who may not be quite ready or interested. The heart of a person who does not have a personal relationship with Jesus may also be closed, hard or encumbered. I encourage you to still deliver the gift of blessing as led by the Holy Spirit because miracles do happen!

- **Hard heart:** The blessing falls on stony ground without much depth of earth, so it does not take root.

- **Encumbered heart:** The blessing falls on thorny ground and begins to spring up, but is eventually choked out.

- **Good heart:** The blessing falls on good ground and yields an increasing harvest of transformation.

Ask the Holy Spirit to help you discern the heart condition of recipients while you are crafting the blessing, and before you begin speaking. You will have an even better sense during the delivery of the blessing and afterwards. This is where the partnership between prayer and blessing is so critical. Prayer work is required after a blessing. God's grace is the divine influence that works upon a heart to change it, and you can pray for the supernatural power of grace to be released into the heart in the measure that is needed. Whenever you sense resistance, you can fasten your faith to the promise of Ezekiel 11:19 and pray into that promise even after you have left the company of the recipient(s):

And I will give them singleness of heart and put a new spirit within them. I will take away their stony, stubborn heart and give them a tender, responsive heart (NLT).

The following is a short, heartfelt blessing from Terry and Melissa Bone:

May your prayers condition the spiritual atmosphere.

May your faith remove mountains of resistance.

May your desires be granted as you make godly declarations for the people you love.[40]

I bless you on this milestone of completing your journey of discovery and bless you even more as you embark on your journey of recovery.

May God bless the fruit of your mouth and may He grant you the joy of a bountiful harvest.

Part 2

RECOVERY

He will give a crown of beauty for ashes,
a joyous blessing instead of mourning.
Isaiah 61:3a NLT

Chapter 12

Blessing Recovery Clinic

Welcome to the Blessing Recovery Clinic! Your birthright family blessings have been waiting for you and I am delighted that you are here to receive them. As you know, they cover the seven major life stages of your development. You can decide how you wish to have them "delivered" to you—all at once, or stage by stage. You also have the option of "self-delivery," which is the route I took because of how eager I was to recover what I had missed. This option is like Jabez going directly to God and asking God to bless him in order to remedy the unhealthy name that had been given to him at birth (see 1 Chronicles 4:9-10). Or, you may ask your parent, spouse, pastor or other mature believer in Christ to deposit these blessing treasures into your heart.

There is no right or wrong way. Be free to choose the options or combination of options that work best for you. The Holy Spirit is your Helper and He will guide you.

Optimizing Your Clinic Experience

You may recall reading about the envelope exercise in Chapter Five. I would encourage you to add this practical piece to your clinic experience. Here are some other points to consider that will help you get the most out of your Blessing Recovery Clinic:

1. Review the chart at the end of the chapter to familiarize yourself with the seven life stages, the question and the fruit of the Spirit associated with each stage. Review the chart with an aim to also

have your spirit identify for you the stage(s) where you need to receive the largest blessing deposit. Concentrate more on those stages during the blessing impartation.

2. Read Chapter Eleven and be sure to audibly pray the prayer of repentance and deliverance.
3. Ask the Holy Spirit to recondition the soil of your heart so that it is good ground.
4. Have some tissue handy, you'll likely need it.
5. Soft background instrumental harp or piano music may enhance your experience.
6. Remember to engage your spirit as primary receptor.
7. During the impartation, envision yourself in the heavenly Father's loving embrace. Just as Jacob laid his hand on the head of Ephraim, see the right hand of the Father on your head. This is the promise in Proverbs 10:6—"Blessings are on the head of the righteous."
8. Don't rush through the impartation. Follow the lead of your spirit and take *Selah* breaks along the way.
9. Water the deposit of blessing seeds sown in your heart with prayer and expect a harvest. Your spirit will register a change almost instantly. However, it may take time for the fruit of the blessing to become evident in your soul. Don't be discouraged. Remember that seeds sown in good ground always produce a harvest as Matthew 13 tells us; "some thirty, some sixty, and some a hundred-fold." When you see what may look like a thirty-fold or lesser harvest, remain steadfast in faith and expect more.
10. Return to the clinic for regular check-ups.

Experiencing the Power of the Blood of Jesus

The Blessing Recovery Clinic is remedial and redemptive in nature and the blood of Jesus is essential for the process. Instead of including the blood as one of the blessing essentials in Chapter Nine, it was intentionally saved for this point to facilitate your understanding of its time-defying power in the context of the Recovery Clinic.

Many of the blessings include the expression, "holding the blood,"[41] upon some aspects of your past. Think of a healing poultice applied to a wound and you'll get the principle. There is no greater poultice or elixir than the blood of Jesus. The concept of holding also has to do with perseverance. Your spirit and the Holy Spirit are not limited by time and space, and neither is the blood of Jesus. You may have sang many times about the blood reaching to the highest mountain and flowing to the lowest valley. Well, here in the Recovery Clinic, you are going to personally experience the unstoppable power of the blood of Jesus as it heals inner wounds that you may have thought were unreachable and incurable.

You'll also want to remember this powerful revelation from Andrew Murray: "God has so inseparably bound together the Holy Spirit and the blood that we may rely on Him to make the power of the blood ceaselessly effective in us by the power of the Spirit."[42]

By the blood of Jesus, the spotless Lamb of God, and by the word of your testimony you shall indeed overcome and have a blessed future (see Revelation 12:11).

> *Every spiritual blessing in the heavenly realm has already been lavished upon [you] as a love gift from [your] wonderful heavenly Father, the Father of our Lord Jesus—all because he sees [you] wrapped into Christ… (Ephesians 1:3 TPT).*

I bless you with an open heart to possess your heavenly Father's blessings with thanksgiving.

The wait is over!

Major Life Stages and Questions[43]

Life Stages		Major Life Questions	Evidence when Blessing Received	Evidence when Blessing Missed	Fruit of the Spirit[44]
1	Conception	Am I welcome in this world?	Belonging Acceptance	Rejection Approval-seeking	Love
2	Pre-born life	Is there a safe place for me in the world?	Safety	Fear	Peace
3	Birth	Will my needs be met in this world?	Provision	Neediness Discontentment	Joy
4	Infancy & childhood	Who can I trust in this world?	Trust Security	Insecurity Mistrust	Gentleness Kindness
5	Teen years	Do I have what it takes to make it in this world? **Male**: Will I be able to impress someone? **Female**: Who will find me lovely? Will I be able to capture someone's attention?	Self-esteem Self-worth Maturity Confidence	Low self esteem Inferiority Inadequacy Low achievement	Patience Self-control
6	Adult years	What am I called to do in this world? Who will share my journey?	Purpose Love Relationship	Experimentation Frustration Inadequacy Unfulfilled Loneliness	Goodness Faithfulness
7	Senior years	Am I still needed in this world?	Value Worth Belonging	Despair Loneliness	Love Peace, Joy Gentleness Kindness Patience Self-control Goodness Faithfulness

Chapter 13

Your Day of Conception

Life Question:
Am I welcome in this world?

Fruit of the Spirit:
Love

Beloved child of the Most High God, I call your spirit to attention to receive the blessing of your Heavenly Father for your day of conception.

Listen with your spirit and receive the answer to the question your spirit has been asking: "Am I welcome in this world?"

Beloved child, we bless the day of your conception, that glorious day on which God, your Heavenly Father, transferred your spirit from the womb of His mind in eternity to the womb of your mother in time. In case your spirit did not sense it then, we celebrate your conception with a hearty welcome: "Welcome to your place on earth."

With the blood of Jesus, we consecrate the egg and the sperm that formed you. We bless you with freedom from any rejection, apprehension or uncertainty your spirit may have picked up at conception, and with the blood of Jesus we flush out all such chemical and cellular memories.

We hold the blood of Jesus over the moment of your conception and separate you from any ungodly bloodline transfers. Instead, we bless you even more with recovery of the rich treasury of generational blessings that God intended to flow to you. We bless you to deepen the treasures in your lifetime and pass an even greater measure to future generations.

In spite of any negative circumstances that may have surrounded your conception, we announce to you that you are not a mistake. You are not an accident. God, your heavenly Father, planned for you to be here. "Out of the hundreds of millions of possible combinations from your parents' DNA, God determined that you would be you." [45] So, we call your spirit now into a celebration of God's choices and design for you in personhood, sexuality, family relationships, time, and place.

We bless you with God-ordained identity, destiny, purpose and resources. We bless you with a secure consciousness of your acceptance and belonging.

Listen again with your spirit and receive the Holy Spirit's impartation of the fruit of LOVE from the Father's heart to your spirit…Hear the words of your heavenly Father:

- Beloved child, I am your heavenly Father. I am the very Source of your life, and I knew you before you were conceived in your mother's womb.

- In love, I drew you out of Myself and stamped My perfect image upon you.

- In love, I proclaimed over you at creation, "Very Good!"

- Even when sin came between us, I did not abandon My love for you. In mercy, I redeemed you through Jesus because of My great love for you.

- Nothing can change the fact that I created you in love, by love, and for love.

- As I love Jesus, so have I loved you. In Jesus, I lavished My love upon you.

- "See what great love the Father has lavished on [you], that [you] should be called [a child] of God! That is what [you] are!"

- In the natural you may not have known the tender joy of being loved by your biological father. Today, will you allow the sufficiency of My perfect love to fill up all that is missing, wipe away every tear and heal every pain?

- Beloved one, I call you deeper into My love. Come home to My love! Believe, receive, and experience My perfect love for you.

- Today, you have found the love you have been seeking all your life.

- Be strengthened in your inner being by the refreshing streams of My Spirit of Love. Be deeply rooted in My love and be founded securely in My love.

- As of this day, My child, may you always experience My extravagant, unfailing love as the bedrock of your life. You are My beloved![46]

Now take a moment to deposit LOVE into your heart and give thanks to the Father.

INSTRUCTION: *IF YOU ARE DOING THE ENVELOPE EXERCISE, PUT THE WORD LOVE IN YOUR ENVELOPE AT THE END OF THIS PRAYER.*

Dear Heavenly Father, I accept Your gracious word.
Yes, I believe that because You chose for me to be here, I am welcome on the earth!
Thank You for Your extravagant, unfailing love that is the bedrock of my life.
I rest in Your unfailing love, Father.

Amen.

Chapter 14

Your Pre-Born Life

Life Question:
Is there a safe place for me in this world?

Fruit of the Spirit:
Peace

Beloved child of the Most High God, I call your spirit to attention to receive the blessing of your heavenly Father for your pre-born life in your mother's womb.

Listen with your spirit and receive the answer to the question your spirit has been asking: "Is there a safe place for me in this world?"

Beloved child, we bless your pre-born life and each day that your body was wonderfully woven together in your mother's womb by the hand of God, your heavenly Father. "Lo, it is written of you, a body He has prepared for you"—a body uniquely crafted and specially designed to fulfill the specific purpose for which God created you. "Wonderfully made," "Masterpiece," are the signature seals your heavenly Father has placed upon you.

The environment of the womb in which you were nurtured may have left you uncertain about the safety of the world into which you were born. We now release the flow of the blood of Jesus into each day that you were in the womb and saturate you with the peace of God's presence. We hold the blood of Jesus upon any experience, word, thought or emotion that may have caused you to feel unsafe, and we release the cleansing power of the blood upon any root of fear and unhealthy memory.

Today, we bless you with a deep consciousness that "God has provided and will always provide a safe place for you, a place of refuge on this earth from the forces that may set themselves against you."[47] There is indeed a safe place for you in the very presence of your heavenly Father: in the palm of His hands, and under the shadow of His wings.

In the name of Jesus Christ of Nazareth, we bless you with the completion of all essential nurturing and bonding ordained by God for your spirit, soul, and body during your pre-born days. We bless you into the renewal of wholesome brain connections for sound mental health and emotional fortitude. We bless your physical body with soundness and strength for all the days of your life. We bless you with strength in your innermost being. May your spirit grow to be strong and take the lead over your soul and body according to God's design.

Listen again with your spirit and receive the Holy Spirit's impartation of the fruit of PEACE from the Father's heart to your spirit...Hear the words of your heavenly Father:

- My beloved child, I watched you as you were being formed and woven together in the womb. I saw you even before you were born and recorded every day of your life in My book. I laid out every moment before a single day came into being. My thoughts about you are precious. You can't even count them, for they outnumber the grains of sand.

- I am your Jehovah Shalom, and today, I say to you, "Peace, do not be afraid!" In Me, you are safe. Yes, My child, in Me, you are secure. Like a blanket, My peace has covered you in the womb and will cover you all the days of your life.

- I have ordained peace for you—completeness, wholeness, wellness and prosperity all the days of your life.

- More than that, I have covenanted Myself to you in peace. Listen to these words I spoke through My Prophet Isaiah and let them be your anchor: "The mountains may depart and the hills may be removed, but My covenant of peace will not be removed because of My mercy."
- In My Son, Jesus, you have the full expression of My enduring peace. Listen to His words; receive them into your heart and spirit: "I leave the gift of peace with you—My peace. Not the kind of fragile peace given by the world, but My perfect peace. Don't yield to fear or be troubled in your hearts—instead, be courageous!"
- I have told you these things so that in Me, you may have peace.
- Let My perfect and extravagant love for you replace every fear.
- Receive now My PEACE as your sure foundation and as the stability of your times. [48]
- Receive in the Name of Jesus Christ of Nazareth.

Now take a moment to deposit PEACE into your heart and give thanks to the Father.

INSTRUCTION: *IF YOU ARE DOING THE ENVELOPE EXERCISE, PUT THE WORD PEACE IN YOUR ENVELOPE AT THE END OF THIS PRAYER.*

Dear Heavenly Father, I accept Your gracious word.
Yes, I believe that I am safe in Your watchful care.
Thank You that Your covenant of peace will never fail.
I rest in Your perfect peace, Father.

Amen.

Chapter 15

YOUR DAY OF BIRTH

LIFE QUESTION:
WILL MY NEEDS BE MET IN THIS WORLD?

FRUIT OF THE SPIRIT:
JOY

Beloved child of the Most High God, I call your spirit to attention to receive the blessing of your heavenly Father for your day of birth.

Listen with your spirit and receive the answer to the question your spirit has been asking: "Will my needs be met in this world?"

Beloved child, we bless and joyfully celebrate the day of your birth. Oh, how the earth and all of heaven rejoiced at your birth! Angels heralded the news of your birth and your star shone brightly in the sky, announcing the time and place of your arrival.

We bless you into a sustained consciousness of this joyous celebration each day of your life, especially at your birthday milestones. Neither the passing of the years nor the experiences of life will diminish the value of your presence on earth. We bless your birth order in the family to which God sent you. We bless you with the knowledge that you are rightly positioned for the purposes of God.

As you left the familiar surroundings of your mother's womb where your physical needs were automatically met, you entered a strange and possibly even uncomfortable physical environment, and the question of whether your needs would continue to be met may have loomed large in your spirit.

Today, we bless you with the full assurance that your needs will always be met by the rich supply of your heavenly Father, the One who planned for you to be here. It is He who feeds the birds of the air and adorns the flowers of the field; how much more will He care for you? Indeed, you are far more precious to your heavenly Father.

We hold the blood of Jesus upon your birth experiences and any words that may have left you with a sense of neediness and discontentment. In the Name of Jesus Christ of Nazareth, we bless you with an overflowing supply of all needs, and with healthy spiritual discernment to process the world around you.

We invoke the blessing of God's favor on the names chosen for you as well as the family name into which you were born. May you fulfill the godly identity, destiny and heritage associated with each name!

Listen again with your spirit and receive the Holy Spirit's impartation of the fruit of JOY from the Father's heart to your spirit…Hear the words of your heavenly Father:

- My dear child, you are My bundle of joy, and I long for you to share in the joy that My heart feels toward you. "I take delight in you with gladness…I rejoice over you with joyful songs."
- In eternity past, I set apart the day of your birth. It is your day!
- All your days are ordained by Me, so rejoice and be glad in each one of them.
- I have no greater joy than to know that you are walking in the truth about who I am and who you are. When you walk in truth you honor Me.
- I have planned for you to experience different kinds of joy in your journey through life.

- Know, however, My child, that you must come again and again into My presence to find fullness of joy and sustaining pleasures.
- Listen to what I spoke concerning you through My Prophet Isaiah: "I have given you a crown of beauty for ashes, a joyous blessing instead of mourning, festive praise instead of despair. In the righteousness that is from Me, you will be like a great oak planted by Me for My own glory."
- "I have told you these things so that you will be filled with My joy. Yes, your joy will overflow!"
- Indeed, I have anointed your head with the oil of joy and your cup I have filled to the point that it is overflowing.
- My joy is your strength. "Go out now in joy and be led forth in peace; the mountains and hills will burst into song before you, and all the trees of the field will clap their hands."
- Receive My fruit of JOY as the baseline of your life to which you return time and time again. [49]
- Receive in the Name of Jesus Christ of Nazareth.

Now take a moment to deposit JOY into your heart and give thanks to the Father.

INSTRUCTION: *IF YOU ARE DOING THE ENVELOPE EXERCISE, PUT THE WORD JOY IN YOUR ENVELOPE AT THE END OF THIS PRAYER.*

Dear Heavenly Father, I accept Your gracious word.
Yes, I believe that all my needs are met by You.
Thank You for YOUR joy as the baseline of my life to which I return again and again.
I rest in Your fullness of joy, Father.
Amen.

Chapter 16

Your Infancy and Childhood

Life Question: Who can I trust in this world?

Fruit of the Spirit: Gentleness & Kindness

Beloved child of the Most High God, I call your spirit to attention to receive the blessing of your heavenly Father for your infancy and childhood.

Listen with your spirit and receive the answer to the question your spirit has been asking: "Who can I trust in this world?"

Beloved child, we bless your years of infancy and childhood. Today, as Jesus blessed the little children while on earth, He picks you up in His arms and speaks gentle, kind, loving words of blessing to you. He lets you know how valuable and precious you are to Him.

He blesses you with a healthy view of life to process your early experiences and your relationships with your family and others. He blesses your spiritual, mental, emotional, intellectual and physical growth with the provision of all that God intended for you as a secure foundation on which to grow.

We hold the blood of Jesus upon any experience of abuse, dishonor, emotional injury, harsh or excessive discipline that may have short-circuited your capacity to trust others or even to trust God. We release the cleansing power of His blood upon all unhealthy memories, especially at the subconscious level.

For the sake of your own freedom, may you now receive God's supernatural grace to grant forgiveness for any neglect, abandonment, or harm done to you intentionally or unintentionally. We apply the healing balm of the blood of Jesus upon any unhealed hurts and call forth your full restoration.

We bless the seed of God's Word in your heart to shape your character, mindset, and moral values. We bless your spirit with increased passion for the presence of the Lord and a heightened sensitivity to His voice. Even as a child, may you, like Samuel, hear and honor the voice of God, and may you speak on His behalf as Samuel did.

Listen again with your spirit and receive the Holy Spirit's impartation of the fruit of GENTLENESS & KINDNESS from the Father's heart to your spirit...Hear the words of your heavenly Father:

- Comfort, comfort, My child, as I speak tenderly to you and tell you that your sad days are gone.
- "I empower you [now] for victory with My wrap-around presence. My power within makes you strong...and by stooping down in gentleness, I strengthen you and make you great."
- "My greatness is unsearchable and so is yours."
- "I am rich in kindness and grace...and have showered My kindness on you along with all wisdom and understanding."
- My merciful kindness towards you is great, because I love you very much.
- Receive My fruit of GENTLENESS and KINDNESS and let them grow in you as expressions of My image in you. [50]

- Receive in the Name of Jesus Christ of Nazareth.

Now take a moment to deposit GENTLENESS and KINDNESS into your heart and give thanks to the Father.

INSTRUCTION: *IF YOU ARE DOING THE ENVELOPE EXERCISE, PUT THE WORDS GENTLENESS AND KINDNESS IN YOUR ENVELOPE AT THE END OF THIS PRAYER.*

Dear Heavenly Father, I accept Your gracious word.
Yes, I believe that I can trust in You with all my heart.
Thank You for Your gentleness and loving kindness that are taking root in my spirit even now.
I rest in Your gentleness and kindness, Father.

Amen.

Chapter 17

Your Teen Years

Life Question:
Do I have what it takes to make it in this world?

Fruit of the Spirit:
Patience & Self-Control

Beloved son/daughter of the Most High God, I call your spirit to attention to receive the blessing of your heavenly Father for your teen years.

Listen with your spirit and receive the answer to the question your spirit has been asking: "Do I have what it takes to make it in this world?"

Beloved son/daughter, we bless your teen years as you transition from being a child into a season of apprenticeship for adulthood. We bless your rite of passage with the recovery and filling by the Holy Spirit of every provision that God ordained for you to have. As it was said of Jesus, may you increase in wisdom, in maturity and in favor with God and the people around you!

We bless you into a secure consciousness and confident assurance that God has designed you and provided everything you need to handle the greater responsibilities of life. You have what it takes to excel in all spheres of life: spiritually, morally, socially, psychologically, intellectually, financially and physically.

[For teen boys only] Yes, God's image is stamped upon you, and you have what it takes to make it as a great man of God.

[For teen girls only] Yes, you have what it takes to make it as a great woman of God. God's image is stamped upon you, and you are lovely, inside and out.

In the Name of Jesus Christ of Nazareth, and by the power of His blood and saving grace, we call you to surrender any belief or mindset motivated by the spirit of the world. Your self-evaluation is not based on the world's standards, but on the standard of your heavenly Father who used His divine power to put you together.

May the blood of Jesus free you from any guilt or shame associated with behaviors, choices, and experiences in your teen years that were contrary to the ways of God and His purpose for your life. In particular, we hold the blood of Jesus on your brain for the rooting out of any learned responses or memories that could be detrimental. May you experience supernatural renewal in any area of the brain that needs to be set right!

We bless you with God-appointed relationships to "mentor you in character and in your life's calling." [51] We bless you even more with a deepening relationship with the Holy Spirit as your Teacher. May He guide you into all truth! You shall be taught by Him and great shall be your peace.

"Whether you turn to the right or left, your ears will hear a voice, saying, 'This is the way, walk in it.' He awakens you morning by morning. He awakens your ear to listen like one being instructed. Morning by morning, He shall open your ears to hear like one being taught."

Listen again with your spirit and receive the Holy Spirit's impartation of the fruit of PATIENCE & SELF-CONTROL from the Father's heart to your spirit…Hear the words of your heavenly Father:

- My child, I made everything that concerns you beautiful in its time. Your times are in My hands.

- I chose you for your generation. I marked out your appointed time in history, and where you would live to serve My purpose in your generation. I take great delight in you and have given you My joy as your strength to carry out the purpose that I have for you.
- "Have you not known? Have you not heard? The everlasting God, the Lord, The Creator of the ends of the earth, neither faints nor is weary. His understanding is unsearchable. He gives power to the weak, and to those who have no might He increases their strength. [Even youths become weak and tired, and young men fall in exhaustion]. But those who wait on the Lord shall renew their strength; they shall mount up with wings like eagles, they shall run and not be weary, they shall walk and not faint."
- "Wait and hope for and expect the Lord; be brave and of good courage and let your heart be stout and enduring. Yes, wait for and hope for and expect the Lord."
- Wait by entwining yourself to Me, like a vine wrapped around a tree. Then patience will have its perfect work, and you will be perfect and complete, lacking nothing.
- I have given you My Spirit of self-control to free you from impulsiveness. Do not fear, for you can do all things through Christ who strengthens you.
- Receive My fruit of PATIENCE & SELF-CONTROL, for they synchronize your life with heaven's perfect timing in everything that concerns you. [52]
- Receive in the Name of Jesus Christ of Nazareth.

Now take a moment to deposit PATIENCE and SELF-CONTROL into your heart and give thanks to the Father.

INSTRUCTION: *IF YOU ARE DOING THE ENVELOPE EXERCISE, PUT THE WORDS PATIENCE AND SELF-CONTROL IN YOUR ENVELOPE AT THE END OF THIS PRAYER.*

Dear Heavenly Father, I accept Your gracious word.
Yes, I believe that I have what it takes to make it in my generation.
Thank You that Your gifts of patience and self-control are at work in my heart and life even now.
I rest in your patience and self-control, Father.

Amen.

Chapter 18

Your Adult Years

Life Question:
What am I called to do in this world and who will share my journey?

Fruit of the Spirit:
Goodness and Faithfulness

Beloved son/daughter of the Most High God, I call your spirit to attention to receive the blessing of your heavenly Father for your adult years.

Listen with your spirit and receive the answer to the question your spirit has been asking: "What am I called to do in this world and who will share my journey?"

Beloved son/daughter, we bless your adult identity and destiny. May your spirit be strong to follow the lead of the Holy Spirit, and may you mature into your spiritual identity as one of the glorious sons and daughters that the world is yearning to see unveiled.

We bless your roles and responsibilities in your family, in the church, in the marketplace, and in the larger community. May you discover and fulfill the purpose for which God sent you here on the earth, and may you be a witness of God's authority and power in your assigned spheres of influence.

May you discover and use your unique gifts, talents, and abilities to the honor and glory of God who entrusted them to you. May you also take hold of every kind of resource that God has provided for you in the spiritual, relational, physical, and financial realms. May you carry the fragrance of Christ to attract to yourself every kind of relationship that God has ordained for you, and to dispel those that are not of Him.

"May the Father of Glory...impart into you the riches of the Spirit of wisdom and the Spirit of revelation to know Him through your deepening intimacy. May the light of God illuminate the eyes of your imagination, flooding you with light, until you experience the full revelation of the hope of His calling…and the immeasurable greatness of God's power made available to you through faith."

We hold the blood of Jesus upon every experience and against every spiritual force that would seek to hinder your progress or block the blessing of God from flowing in your life. May you experience the victorious power of the blood of Jesus Christ in every area of your life!

Listen again with your spirit and receive the Holy Spirit's impartation of the fruit of GOODNESS & FAITHFULNESS from the Father's heart to your spirit…Hear the words of your heavenly Father:

- My beloved son/daughter, "O taste and see that I am good. You are blessed as you take refuge in My goodness. For the Lord is good and His love endures forever; [My] faithfulness continues through all generations."

- Yes, from generation to generation, I am God. I chose you for your generation, carefully marking out your appointed time in history and your dwelling place.

- I bless you today with My generational heart and vision so that you may serve My purpose in your generation. Tell the next generation of My great marvels—My miracles and power that have brought you this far.

- Surely, My goodness and mercy shall follow you all the days of your life as you fulfill My purpose that is wrapped up in you.

- You are complete in Christ, and in Him you find the rich treasures of My goodness. In Him, I have demonstrated My faithfulness to you.
- My loving kindness indeed never ceases. My compassion never fails. They are new every morning. Great is My faithfulness.
- So, My beloved, greet each moment, each new day, even each year with great anticipation of the good things I have in store for you.
- **[For men only]** I bless you today, My beloved son, and affirm you as one in whom I am well pleased. Receive My Spirit of Fatherhood, for I am the perfect Father in whom you find your Source to be the kind of father I ordained you to be, both as a natural and spiritual father.
- **[For women only]** I bless you today, My beloved daughter, and affirm you as one in whom I am well pleased. Allow My Spirit to fill every dimension of your life and the lives of your family members, for I am the perfect Father in whom every family finds its Source.
- My beloved sons and daughters, receive now the fruit of My GOODNESS and FAITHFULNESS, for it is I who have begun a good work in you and I am faithful to bring it to completion. [53]
- Receive in the Name of Jesus Christ of Nazareth.

Now take a moment to deposit GOODNESS and FAITHFULNESS into your heart and give thanks to the Father.

INSTRUCTION: *IF YOU ARE DOING THE ENVELOPE EXERCISE, PUT THE WORDS GOODNESS AND FAITHFULNESS IN YOUR ENVELOPE AT THE END OF THIS PRAYER.*

Dear Heavenly Father, I accept Your gracious word.
Yes, I believe that You have purposely placed me here to represent Your kingdom in my circle of influence. I believe that I am blessed with healthy relationships of every kind.
Thank You for Your gifts of goodness and faithfulness that never fail.
I rest in Your goodness and faithfulness, Father.

Amen.

Chapter 19

YOUR SENIOR YEARS

LIFE QUESTION:
AM I STILL NEEDED IN THIS WORLD?

FRUIT OF THE SPIRIT:
LOVE, PEACE, JOY, GENTLENESS, KINDNESS,PATIENCE, SELF-CONTROL, GOODNESS, FAITHFULNESS

[If you are not yet in your senior years, receive this blessing as a time-released blessing capsule for your senior years.]

Beloved son/daughter of the Most High God, I call your spirit to attention to receive the blessing of your heavenly Father for your senior years.

Listen with your spirit and receive the answer to the question your spirit has been asking: "Am I still needed in this world?"

Beloved son/daughter, we bless your senior years with a secure consciousness that indeed you are still needed in this world. We bless you with a revelation that your very presence on earth is God's affirmation that there still remains something significant for you to do. Whether it is the finishing of your assigned purpose, the fulfillment of a dream, the healing of your generational history, or seeing God's righteousness, justice, and order manifested in you and your loved ones, we bless you with the grace to finish strong. May you have strength like Caleb to possess the full inheritance that God has allotted to you!

Today, we honor you for your many years of selfless service to your family and others. We gratefully recognize and bless your contribution to the Kingdom of God. May you be sought out for wisdom and counsel so that the benefit of your hard-earned insights can be passed on to others! We bless your legacy of righteousness as a rich treasure that generations to come will build upon.

We acknowledge that your journey through the years may have been difficult at times, and we thank God for His sovereign power in taking those things that Satan meant for evil and using them for good. We hold the blood of Jesus upon any lingering imprints of emotional pain and release its redemptive power into the timeline of your life to heal, restore and fill all that may be missing, wounded or broken. We bless and insulate your brain with the blood of Jesus for excellent cognitive health all your days, in the Name of Jesus Christ of Nazareth.

For the remaining time that you are on earth, we bless you to grow in grace and to go from glory to glory. "May you never be without the presence of the Holy Spirit. May your heart always be at peace. May your mind always be alert and learning. May your strength match your days. May God keep you in His love at all times. We bless your memories, so that you may recall the goodness of God and the great times you have had with family and friends."[54]

We bless you with sustaining peace as you trust in your heavenly Father who has numbered your days and will receive your spirit back to Himself, not a day early and not a day late.

We bless you in the Name of Jesus Christ of Nazareth.

Listen again with your spirit and receive the Holy Spirit's impartation of the cumulative harvest of the Fruit of the Spirit from the Father's heart to your spirit...Hear the words of your heavenly Father:

- My beloved son/daughter, you are planted in My presence, and you will flourish continuously. "You will still bear fruit in old age. You will be fresh and flourishing, declaring My uprightness; that I am your rock and there is no unrighteousness in Me."

- At every stage and season of your life, I planted the fruit of My Spirit into your spirit: My extravagant **love** at your conception; My enduring **peace** over your pre-born life; My exuberant **joy** at your birth; My comforting **gentleness** and **kindness** during your infancy and childhood; My treasures of **patience** and **self-control** in your teen years; and My ever-present **goodness** and **faithfulness** in your adult years.

- Indeed, you are like a tree planted by the rivers of water. I have blessed you in this season to bring forth a rich harvest from the fruit of My Spirit that I have sown in you.

- I am "Faithful and True" to the very end.

- "Even to your old age and gray hairs, I am He, [It is I] who will sustain you. I have made you and I will carry you; I will sustain you and I will rescue you."

- I received the prayer of the Psalmist on your behalf, and I have answered. "So, now, when you are old and gray-headed, I, Your God, will not forsake you. I will sustain you that you may show My strength to this generation, and My power to everyone that is to come."

- Today, I bless you with the revelation of knowing that My faithfulness to keep every gracious promise I've made "passes from parents, to children, to grandchildren and beyond."[55]

- Receive in the Name of Jesus Christ of Nazareth.

Now take a moment and give thanks to the Father for the deposit all of the fruit of the Spirit into your heart.

Dear Heavenly Father, I accept Your gracious word.
Yes, I believe that I am still needed in this world.
Thank You for blessing me with the full measure of the Fruit of Your Spirit.
Father, I rest in Your love, peace, joy, gentleness, kindness, patience, self-control, goodness and faithfulness. Yes, I rest in you, my God and my Father.

Amen.

Chapter 20

Glorious Thanksgiving

Heavenly Father, you have honored me with your manifold blessings, not because of what I did or did not do, but because of all that Jesus Christ of Nazareth, my Redeemer, has accomplished for me. I have been giving thanks at each border crossing of my life, in response to each recovered blessing. Now, the crescendo—Glorious Thanksgiving!!!

Your Word written through the Psalmist draws me to this place of glorious, passionate thanksgiving for all You have done for me.

Psalm 118 - The Passion Translation
Glorious Thanksgiving

Keep on giving your thanks to God, for he is so good!
His constant, tender love lasts forever!
2 *Let all his princely people sing,*
"His constant, tender love lasts forever!"
3 *Let all his holy priests sing,*
"His constant, tender love lasts forever!"
4 *Let all his lovers who bow low before him sing,*
"His constant, tender love lasts forever!"
5 *Out of my deep anguish and pain I prayed,*
and God, you helped me as a father.
You came to my rescue and broke open the way
into a beautiful and broad place.
6 *Now I know, Lord, that you are for me,*
and I will never fear what man can do to me.

Thank You, heavenly Father, for Your constant, tender, everlasting love for me. Thank You for the beautiful and broad place into which You have launched me.

Now, Father, in the Name of Jesus Christ of Nazareth, I ask that Your covenant blood and the seal of the Holy Spirit would be upon the blessings I have recovered for all eternity.

To You be all the glory throughout all generations forever and ever.

Amen.

Afterword

It has been said, "The heart and soul of the Christian life is learning to hear God's voice and developing the courage to do what He asks us to do." Rev. Marva Tyndale has encountered the presence of the Lord and she has heard the voice of God concerning the principle of **"The Blessing Birthright."**

This book is indeed a delightful guide that is full of important information. It is for those who seek a greater understanding of the mandate to pronounce these blessings. In this book, the author exhibits heart-felt, wise, honest, tender and helpful insights.

If there is a measure of truth in the saying, "Don't leave for tomorrow what you can do today," then Rev. Tyndale's book, *Recover Your Blessing Birthright: Transforming Lives and Culture with the Gift of Words,* is ordered by the Holy Spirit for such a time as this. It cannot be left for tomorrow. In fact, we are compelled by the Word of God, the presence, and power of the Holy Spirit to speak blessings daily over our families, churches, communities and nations.

This book is very timely, and it is by far one of the best written studies I have read on the basic principles of imparting verbal blessings on God's people, young and old. As Men and Women of God, our words do have authority! We must learn how to use our authority to create blessings instead of curses, especially over our younger generation. We are being called by God to bless others, and He will bless those we have invoked His name upon (Numbers 6:22-27).

The book is encouraging and challenging. I believe that it is going to be greatly used by God to revolutionize the Christian Church to understand the power of God's Words—power vocalized by human tongues as a medium for the transformation of lives and culture, with rich blessings, from the womb to the tomb.

Be Blessed, Rev. Tyndale.

— Bishop Dr. Canute B. Blake
Lead Pastor, New Life Covenant Centre
www.newlifecovenantcentre.com

1. **Aaron Früh,** *The Forgotten Blessing: Ancient Words that Heal Generational Wounds* (Grand Rapids: Chosen Books, 2006), 21.
2. *Selah* is a Hebrew word that the Amplified Bible translates as "Pause, and think of that."
3. Früh, *The Forgotten Blessing*, 53.
4. John 1:1.
5. Psalm 45:1.
6. Terry and Melissa Bone, *The Power of Blessing: Discovering Your True Identity and Destiny in Christ* (Burlington, ON: Crossroads Christian Communications, 2004), 6. This book has since been published as part of another book, *The Family Blessing Guidebook: Everything You Need to Know to Have a Blessed Family* (see Bibliography).
7. See Appendix Two.
8. Here are some verses related to this divine order that you may wish to read in different translations for more insight into this biblical truth: Ephesians 1:3, 1 Thessalonians 5:23, 1 Corinthians 2:14, John 6:63.
9. Arthur Burk has many resources on this subject. If you would like further insights visit www.theslg.com.
10. See Galatians 5:22.
11. Bone, *The Power of Blessing*, 6.
12. Früh, *The Forgotten Blessing*, 144.
13. Terry and Melissa Bone, *The Family Blessing Guidebook: Everything You Need to Know to Have a Blessed Family*, (www.powerofblessing.com, 2012), 124.
14. Früh, *The Forgotten Blessing*, 16.
15. Craig Hill, *The Ancient Paths* (Littleton: Family Foundations International, 1992), 37.
16. Bone, *The Power of Blessing*, 38. This is a quotation from Alf Davis, the founder of Agape Healing International.

17. Mary Ruth Swope, *The Power of Blessing Your Children* (New Kensington: Whitaker House, 2010). See Appendix Four for samples.
18. Bone, *The Family Blessing Guidebook*, 37.
19. *Mishpochah*: News from Sid Roth's *It's Supernatural!* Number 1801, January 2018.
20. The YouTube link for *I AM. 365 Names of God* is https://www.youtube.com/watch?v=8UQf9zZBzv4.
21. Frances J. Roberts, *Come Away My Beloved* (Uhrichsville: Barbour Publishing Inc., 2002), 156, 159.
22. See Warren M. Marcus' *Prayer of the Priestly Blessing: Amplified Hebrew to English Interpretation* in Appendix Three.
23. Bill Gothard, *The Power of Spoken Blessings* (Oak Brook: Institute in Basic Life Principles, 2003) 17. Althouse, Ann. (March 18, 2013). "*The original meaning of the word "bless" is about blood.*" Retrieved January 22, 2018 from http://althouse.blogspot.ca/2013/03/the-original-meaning-of-word-bless-is.html.
24. Bone, *The Family Blessing Guidebook*, 133.
25. Ibid., 163-164.
26. Ibid., 28.
27. Stephen R. Covey, *The 7 Habits of Highly Effective People: Powerful Lessons in Personal Change* (New York: Simon & Schuster, 1989)
28. Bone, *The Family Blessing Guidebook*, 130.
29. Bill Gothard, *The Power of Spoken Blessings (*Sisters: Multnomah Publishers, Inc., 2004).
30. Bone, *The Family Blessing Guidebook*, 38-39.
31. Arthur Burk, *Ministering to Babies in the Womb* (https://theslg.com/cd-albums).
32. A sample is included in Appendix Four. An excellent resource is Craig Hill, *Bar Barakah: A Parent's Guide to a Christian Bar Mitzvah* (Littleton: Family Foundations International, 1998).

33. A copy of the Chaplaincy Blessing is in Appendix Seven, Author's Sample Blessings.
34. Dorothy Astoria, *The Name Book* (Bloomington: Bethany House Publishers, 1997).
35. http://www.7culturalmountains.org/.
36. The House of Good Hope website is https://hartfordprayer.com/prayer-tools/seven-mountains-prayer-points/ (Accessed March 12, 2018).
37. Früh, *The Forgotten Blessing*, 104.
38. See Appendix Four. You may be able to glean some ideas from the summary template created from the chapter entitled "How to Bless Your Household" in Aaron Früh's book, *The Forgotten Blessing.*
39. Reading these passages in The Passion Translation will add depth to the prayer: 1 John 1:9, 2 Corinthians 10:3-5, Matthew 6:9-13, Psalm 51, Psalm 19:14, Psalm 139:24. You may access The Passion Translation online at www.biblegateway.com.
40. Bone, *The Family Blessing Guidebook*, 164.
41. Billye Brim, The *Blood and the Glory* (Tulsa: Harrison House Inc,. 1995), 97.
42. Andrew Murray, *The Blood of the Cross* (New Kensington: Whitaker House, 1981), 9.
43. The source for "Life Stages and Major Life Questions" is Terry and Melissa Bone, *The Family Blessing, 27-32.*
44. See Galatians 5:22.
45. Bone, *The Family Blessing Guidebook*, 168.
46. Jeremiah 1:5, 1 John 3:1; Ephesians 3:17.
47. Bone, *The Family Blessing Guidebook*, 169.
48. Hebrews 10:5, Psalm 139:14. Ephesians 2:10, Psalm 139:14-18 NLT, Judges 6:23; Isaiah 54:10, John 14:27 TPT, John 16:33; Isaiah 33:6.

49. Philippians 4:19, Zephaniah 3:17, Psalm 118:24, Psalm 16:11, 3 John 1:4, Isaiah 61:3 NLT Paraphrased, John 15:11 NLT, Psalms 45, 7b, Psalm 23:5b, Nehemiah 8:10, Isaiah 55:12.
50. Isaiah 40:1 NLT, Psalm 18:35 TPT, Psalm 145:3, Ephesians 1:7-8 NLT, Psalm 117:2.
51. Bone, *The Family Blessing Guidebook*, 171.
52. Luke 2:52, John 16:13, Isaiah 54:13, Isaiah 30:21, Isaiah 50:4, Ecclesiastes 3:11, Psalm 31:15, Acts 17:26, Acts 13:36, Zephaniah 3:17; Nehemiah 8:10, Isaiah 40:28-31 [NIV], Psalm 27:14 AMPC, James 1:4, 2 Timothy 1:7, Philippians 4:13.
53. Romans 8:19 TPT, Ephesians 1:17-19 TPT, Psalm 34:8, Psalm 100:5; Acts 17:26, Acts 13:36, Psalm 23:6, Lamentations 3:23, Philippians 1:6.
54. Adapted from: Bone, *The Family Blessing Guidebook*, 192-193.
55. Joshua 14:6-13, Psalm 92:13-15, Psalm 1:3; Isaiah 46:4; Psalm 71:18, Psalm 103:17b TPT.
56. The source for "Life Stages and Major Life Questions" is Terry and Melissa Bone, *The Family Blessing, 27-32.*
57. Galatians 5:22.
58. Warren M. Marcus, *The Priestly Prayer of the Blessing: The Ancient Secret of the Only Prayer in the Bible Written by God Himself (Lake Mary: Charisma House, 2018)*, 213-217.
59. Bone, *The Family Blessing Guidebook*, 123. Citation from the Sabbath Blessing by Tevye and Golde for their daughters in *Fiddler on the Roof.* From the 1971 film adaptation of the 1964 Broadway Musical of the same name. MGM Studios. Directed by Norman Jewison.
60. Bone, *The Family Blessing Guidebook*, 167-194.
61. Ibid., 160-161.
62. Ibid., 172. Chapter 15: *Rites of Passage at Teen Years.*
63. Früh, *The Forgotten Blessing*, 139-154. This template is extracted

from the chapter on "How to Bless Your Household."

64. Mary Ruth Swope, *The Power of Blessing Your Children* (New Kensington: Whitaker House, 2010).
65. Ibid., 40.
66. Ibid., 69.
67. Ibid., 80.
68. Ibid., 42.
69. Ibid., 41.
70. Sylvia Gunter and Arthur Burk, *Blessing Your Spirit*. (Birmingham: The Father's House, 2005), 1-3
71. Ibid., 147-148.
72. Arthur Burk, *Blessing Your Soul*. (Anaheim: Sapphire Leadership Group, Inc., 2004), 209.
73. Bill Gothard, *The Power of Spoken Blessings*. (Sisters: Multnomah Publishers, Inc., 2004), 86-87.
74. Bone, *The Family Blessing Guidebook*, 163.
75. 2 Corinthians 1:3-4, Ephesians 1:17-23, Ephesians 2:6, Numbers 6:24-27.

Bibliography

Astoria, Dorothy. *The Name Book.* Bloomington: Bethany House Publishers, 1997

Boweya, Andrea. *Legacy Moments.* www.xulonpress.com, 2012

Bone, Terry and Melissa. *The Power of Blessing: Discovering Your True Identity and Destiny in Christ.* Canada, 2004

Bone, Terry and Melissa. *The Family Blessing Guidebook: Everything You Need to Know to Have a Blessed Family.* Canada, 2012

Brim, Billye. *The Blood and The Glory.* Tulsa: Harrison House Inc., 1995

Burk, Arthur. *Blessing Your Soul.* Anaheim: Sapphire Leadership Group, Inc., 2004

Burk, Arthur and Gunther, Sylvia. *Blessing Your Spirit.* Birmingham: The Father's House, 2005

Capps, Charles. *The Tongue, A Creative Force.* Tulsa: Harrison House, Inc., 1976

Früh, Aaron. *The Forgotten Blessing: Ancient Words that Heal Generational Wounds.* Grand Rapids: Chosen Books, 2006

Garborg, Ralph. *The Family Blessing—Covering for Your Family's Future.* (Lakeland: White Stone Books, 2003

Gothard, Bill. *The Power of Spoken Blessings.* Sisters: Multnomah Publishers, Inc., 2004

Gothard, Bill. *The Power of Spoken Blessings.* Oak Brook: Institute in Basic Life Principles, 2003

Hill, Craig. *Bar Barakah: A Parent's Guide to a Christian Bar Mitzvah.* Littleton: Family Foundations International, 1998

Hill, Craig. *The Ancient Paths.* Littleton: Family Foundations International, 1992

Marcus, Warren M. *The Priestly Prayer of the Blessing: The Ancient Secret of the Only Prayer in the Bible Written by God Himself.* Lake Mary: Charisma House, 2018

Murray, Andrew. *The Blood of the Cross.* New Kensington: Whitaker House, 1981

Roberts, Frances J. *Come Away My Beloved.* Uhrichsville: Barbour Publishing Inc., 2002

Smalley, Gary and Trent John. *The Blessing*. Nashville: Thomas Nelson, Inc., 1986

Swope, Mary Ruth. *The Power of Blessing Your Children*. New Kensington: Whitaker House, 2010

CDs & DVDs

Arthur Burk, *Nurturing Your Spirit: Basic Seminar Level 1*. (https://theslg.com/cd-albums).

Arthur Burk, *Ministering to Babies in the Womb*. (https://theslg.com/cd-albums).

Ed Montgomery, *The Blessing Factor*. (www.alcstore.org).

Appendix 1

The Blessing Mantle

The Blessing Mantle

"...I will take some of the Spirit that is upon you,
and I will put the Spirit upon them also..."
Numbers 16:17 NLT

________________________ (your name), I call your spirit to attention in the Name of Jesus Christ of Nazareth to receive your heavenly Father's impartation of the mantle, anointing, and authority of a Blessing Ambassador to you.

- The Spirit of the Lord is upon you. Your heavenly Father has designated you as His representative to minister spoken blessings that will transform lives and your culture. He sets His right hand upon your head, anoints your head with oil, and empowers you for the task ahead.

- In the spirit of Isaiah 58:12, you will be known as a restorer. Yes, you shall be called a restorer of the culture of blessing; the restorer of the ancient paths to which God had invited His people to return in Jeremiah 6:16.

- You are now receiving an infilling of the anointing oil in overflowing measure. This anointing shall gush out of your innermost being, clothe you with the glorified presence of God, and infuse the words you speak with God's supernatural grace and power.

- Your tongue is the pen of a ready writer and you shall write the message of the heavenly Father's enduring love on the hearts of many.

- As the mouthpiece of your heavenly Father, He has blessed you and made you a blessing. Not one of your words shall fall to the ground. His words spoken through you shall prosper wherever they are sent.

- Receive the pronouncement of God's Priestly Blessing upon you:

  "The Lord bless you and keep you;
  The Lord make His face shine upon you, And be gracious to you;
  The Lord lift up His countenance upon you,
  And give you peace."

- With this blessing the Name of God, your heavenly Father, is placed upon you and He Himself blesses you.
- May you be diligent in stirring up every divine gift that is within you.
- Freely you have received, freely you should give.

In the Name of Jesus Christ of Nazareth, this Blessing Mantle is established in you, and the seal of the Holy Spirit is set upon it, now and forever more. Amen.

Appendix 2

Major Life Stages and Questions

Major Life Stages and Questions[56]

Life Stages		Major Life Questions	Evidence when Blessing Received	Evidence when Blessing Missed	Fruit of the Spirit[57]
1	Conception	Am I welcome in this world?	Belonging Acceptance	Rejection Approval-seeking	Love
2	Pre-born life	Is there a safe place for me in the world?	Safety	Fear	Peace
3	Birth	Will my needs be met in this world?	Provision	Neediness Discontentment	Joy
4	Infancy & childhood	Who can I trust in this world?	Trust Security	Insecurity Mistrust	Gentleness Kindness
5	Teen years	Do I have what it takes to make it in this world? **Male**: Will I be able to impress someone? **Female**: Who will find me lovely? Will I be able to capture someone's attention?	Self-esteem Self-worth Maturity Confidence	Low self esteem Inferiority Inadequacy Low achievement	Patience Self-control
6	Adult years	What am I called to do in this world? Who will share my journey?	Purpose Love Relationship	Experimentation Frustration Inadequacy Unfulfilled Loneliness	Goodness Faithfulness
7	Senior years	Am I still needed in this world?	Value Worth Belonging	Despair Loneliness	Love Peace, Joy Gentleness Kindness Patience Self-control Goodness Faithfulness

Appendix 3

Model Blessings

The Priestly Blessing of Numbers 6:24-26

Amplified Hebrew to English Interpretation of Numbers 6:24-26

The Blessing of Ephraim and Manasseh

A Sabbath Blessing from *Fiddler on the Roof*

Model Blessings

THE PRIESTLY BLESSING OF NUMBERS 6:24-26:

"The Lord bless you and keep you;

The Lord make His face shine upon you, And be gracious to you;

The Lord lift up His countenance upon you,

And give you peace."

AMPLIFIED HEBREW TO ENGLISH INTERPRETATION OF NUMBERS 6:24-26[58]

The Lord bless you

May YaHWeh (HE who exists) kneel before you (making Himself available to you as your heavenly Father) so HE can bestow upon you, His promises and gifts.

And keep you

And GUARD YOU with a HEDGE of THORNY PROTECTION that will prevent Satan and all your enemies from harming you. May HE protect your body, soul, mind and spirit, your loved ones and all your possessions.

The Lord make His face shine upon you

May YaHWeh (HE who exists) illuminate the WHOLENESS of HIS BEING toward you, continually bringing to you, order, so that you will fulfill your God-given destiny and purpose.

And be gracious to you

May YaHWeh (HE who exists) provide you with PERFECT LOVE and FELLOWSHIP (never leaving you) and give you SUSTENANCE (provision) and FRIENDSHIP.

The Lord lift His countenance upon you

May YaHWeh (HE who exists) LIFT UP and carry His FULLNESS of being toward you (bringing everything that He has to your aid) supporting YOU with His DIVINE EMBRACE and His ENTIRE BEING.

And give you peace.

May YaHWeh (HE who exists) set in place all YOU need to be WHOLE and COMPLETE so you can walk in victory, moment by moment, by the power of the Holy Spirit. May HE give you supernatural health, peace, welfare, safety, soundness, tranquility, prosperity, perfection, fullness, rest, harmony, as well as, the absence of agitation and discord.

The Extended Blessing of Ephraim and Manasseh from Genesis 48:20; Genesis 41:50-52

May God make you like Ephraim and Manasseh—may He cause you to forget the pain of your past, including the pain of your father's house, and may He make you fruitful and prosperous in the future.

A Sabbath Blessing from *Fiddler on the Roof*[59]

May the Lord protect and defend you.
May He always shield you from shame.
May you come to be
In Israel a shining name.

May God bless you and grant you long lives.
May the Lord fulfill our Sabbath prayer for you.
May God make you good mothers and wives.
May He send you husbands who will care for you.

May the Lord protect and defend you.
May the Lord preserve you from pain.
Favor them, Oh Lord, with happiness and peace.
Oh, hear our Sabbath prayer. Amen.

Appendix 4

List, Guidelines & Samples

List of Sample Blessings
Guidelines for Crafting a Blessing
A Sample Blessing: Rites of Passage
-By Terry and Melissa Bone

Guidelines for Blessing Your Household
-By Aaron Früh

Samples of Blessing Your Children
-By Mary Ruth Swope

Lists, Guidelines & Samples

List of Sample Blessings[60]

Life-Stage Blessings

Pregnancy Blessing (Mom and Baby)

Baby/Child Dedication

Young Child (including name blessing)

New Teen

Wedding

Single Parents

Wedding Anniversary

Middle Years (at age 50)

Retirement

Senior Parents

House Blessing

How to Craft a Blessing for Someone You Know[61]

A blessing has the ability to convey God's favor upon a person when it is crafted with understanding and received with an open heart. Whether spoken or written, the purpose is to recognize and verbalize the noteworthy characteristics of the person, and to articulate what you see God may desire to do in their life and through their life in the future.

To help you get started, try following these steps:

- Prayerfully choose a Scripture that conveys a positive message suitable to the person you wish to bless.
- Write a sentence or two describing something noteworthy that you have observed about this person's actions or character.
- Record words that describe this person's value in your eyes and in the sight of God.
- Add any good thing that you perceive God to be doing in their life right now.
- Describe the ways in which you believe this person can be used by God to encourage and bless others in the future.
- If appropriate, state how you are willing to assist this person to achieve the future you have pictured for him/her.
- Optional: Find the meaning of this person's name and incorporate it into the blessing.

A SAMPLE BLESSING

BAR/BAT BARAKAH CEREMONY SUPPLEMENT.[62]

(Bar/Bat Barakah is the Christian equivalent of the Jewish Bar/Bat Mitzvah).

Today, I call you forth into manhood/womanhood.
You are no longer a child.
You are now an emerging adult.
I am proud to be your father/mother.
You have what it takes to become a man/woman of great character.
You are unconditionally loved and never need to prove your worth or value through your own efforts.
You have everything you need to find and fulfill your destiny.
I commit myself to support you in every way (time, finances, counsel, prayers) during this exciting journey.

GUIDELINES FOR BLESSING YOUR HOUSEHOLD[63]

It is evident that we have a problem. Now, what can we do to solve it and begin a pattern of family life that communicates God's works and wonders from generation to generation? Here are six practical things you can do to bless your household:

1. Plan a special family blessing night.

    a. Parents lay hands on each child individually and bless him/her. "Bless the natural and spiritual strength each one has. Try not to respond to any negative behavior on the child's part, but rather bless the child for what they shall become one day."

    b. Husband blesses the wife according to Proverbs 31:28-31.

c. Wife blesses the husband according to Psalm 128.

2. Bless your romance (the fountain of love in the home between husband and wife).

3. Bless your substance.
   a. Bless all the things you own.
   b. Bless the work of your family's hands.
   c. Bless your land and property.
   d. Bless the womb (if you desire more children).
   e. Bless the Sabbath (a day devoted to rest, relaxation, and spiritual things).
   f. Bless your kitchen pantry.
   g. Bless your future provision and increase.

4. Write a special blessing for special life events (e.g. after a graduation ceremony).

5. Include grandparents in special family times.

6. Share in the Lord's Table together.

Samples of Blessing Your Children[64]

A Controlled Tongue[65]

In the name of Jesus Christ:

I bless your tongue. You will be a person who will learn early in life to weigh your words and measure your thoughts before you pour them forth from your mouth.

Your tongue will speak positive words that affirm and bless those who hear you. Your tongue will always tell the truth in love and will talk to others about good things. Your tongue will constantly find ways to bring happiness to others.

Without fail, your tongue will be used to glorify God and edify your family and friends. It will praise your God all day long.

Proverbs 21:23; Ecclesiastes 3:7; Ephesians 4:15; James 3:4.

Pleasant Words[66]

In the name of Jesus Christ:

I bless you with an understanding of how important it is in life to set a guard over your mouth and to keep watch over the words that come from your lips. You will not speak negative and hurtful words that cause pain and wound spirits.

May you learn quickly that a soft answer turns away wrath and that words thoughtfully spoken bring great rewards with them. You will learn to express pleasant words, profitable advice, and kind speech in all your conversations.

Psalm 141:3; Proverbs 15:23,26; 16:24; 25:11; Luke 6:45; Ephesians 4:29; James 1:19.

Trust[67]

In the name of Jesus Christ:

I bless you with ability to trust in the Lord with all your heart and not depend upon your own understanding. Such trust will keep you on the right track and bring health to your body, as well.

When you trust in the Lord and do good things for others, you can expect Him to meet all your needs and keep you from harm. You will be a happy person.

When you depart from evil and seek peace, the eyes of the Lord are upon you, and His ears are open to your cry. You can trust Him to hear and answer your prayers and give you the desires of your heart.

Psalm 34:8, 37:3-4; Proverbs 3:5, 16:20.

Creativity[68]

In the name of Jesus Christ:

Within you dwells the spirit of creativity, for you are made in the image of the great Creator, the Maker of heaven and earth. He is the One who gives you ideas to design, build, and perform. Let Him fill your imagination with creative thoughts that, when brought to reality, will bring glory to Him and blessings to others.

May the beauty of the Lord our God be upon you to establish the work of your hands.

Genesis 1:26-27; 2 Chronicles 2:12-14; Psalm 90:17, 146:5-6.

Courage[69]

In the name of Jesus Christ:

I bless you with courage to stand in the face of fear and to know that God is your refuge and strength. You do not need to be afraid or terrified, for the Lord your God goes before you; He will never leave you or forsake you.

Every place where you set your foot will be a place of victory for you. No one will be able to stand up against you all the days of your life.

Fear is the opposite of faith, and God has not given you a spirit of fear. He has blessed you with power and love and a sound mind. That is the essence of courage.

Deuteronomy 31:6; Joshua 1:3, 5; 2 Timothy 1:7.

Appendix 5

Samples of Blessing for the Spirit and Soul

Blessing Your Spirit with the Blessings of the Father:
Identity and Legitimacy
Blessing Your Spirit with the Names of God:
Abba Father
Blessing Your Soul:
Legacy
-Arthur Burk

Samples of Blessing for the Spirit and Soul

Blessing Your Spirit with the Blessings of the Father

Identity and Legitimacy[70]

____________(*fill in the name*), I call your spirit to attention in the Name of Jesus Christ of Nazareth. Listen with your spirit to God's Word for you. "For you created my inmost being; you knit me together in my mother's womb. I praise you because I am fearfully and wonderfully made; your works are wonderful, I know that fully well. My frame was not hidden from you when I was made in the secret place. When I was woven together in the depths of the earth, your eyes saw my unformed body. All the days ordained for me were written in your book before one of them came to be" (Psalm 139:13-16).

____________, your Father made you special. You are a very special person, created, crafted and designed by God your Father. Before the foundation of the world, your Father planned for you. You are no accident. You did not have to exist, but your Father willed you into existence. He chose the day and the time you would start your life. He chose your parents and wove you together in your mother's womb. He planned your birth order and put you in your family. He chose every one of your 23 pairs of chromosomes. He chose every one of your 10,000 plus genes. He chose every part of your spiritual heritage. He reached back into your father's bloodline and your mother's bloodline, and from generations past, your heavenly Father chose different parts of your heritage. Some parts are not so beautiful, and some parts are absolutely gorgeous. Yet, your Father wove it all together and gave you everything you need in the package of your life to be an overcomer, a victor, to take the negative parts of your heritage and triumph over them, to walk in the beauty of all that God has placed within you.

Your Father made you beautiful and beloved. I bless you, ___________, because you are fearfully and wonderfully made. God invested an incredible amount of effort and concentration in designing you. You are unique, one of a kind. There is nobody else like you. God has thought extensively about you. Every detail of your body, every organ, and every cell is the result of God's thoughts. Every facet of your personality is the result of His kind intention. You are beautiful, and you are loved. God has blessed you with His love. God smiled on the day He created you. He has been waiting for millennia for the particular point in time when you were conceived. He had great joy in His heart when His plans actually came together. He nurtures your spirit, He watches over you.

Your world needs you. You bring something to your family that no other person has. They need the gifts you bring. Your family would not be complete without you. Others in your circle need the deposit that God has placed in your life.

Your Father wrote your days in His book. He has already read the final chapter, although we have not had that privilege. Your life is not a random thing. He is looking forward to the chapters of the story He has already written. He designed your spiritual heritage. Your generational blessings go back a thousand generations. There is a spiritual treasure chest of generational blessings with your name on it. Those are being released to you incrementally over the course of your life at the appointed, appropriate time. All this is God's master plan. God has foreseen your pain. He promises that because of His love, His power, and His blessing upon you, He causes pain and negative things to be transformed into good things before the end of the story of your life. We don't know everything about who you are going to be or what you are going to do, but you are loved, you are a blessing to your family, and you are a life-giver in the world. You are special, and we celebrate God's miraculous design of who you are. I bless you in the Name of Jesus of Nazareth.

Respond with your spirit…

Write your thoughts, etc.

Blessing Your Spirit with the Names of God

Abba Father[71]

____________(*fill in the name*), I call your spirit to attention in the Name of Abba Father. Read His Word in Galatians 4:6. "Because you are sons, God sent the Spirit of His Son into our hearts, the Spirit who calls out 'Abba, Father.'" God desires you to know Him in many different ways in your life, but one of the most fundamental is to know Him as Abba Father. He desires that you have an intimate relationship with Him as Father, to understand your rights as a child before you walk in your responsibilities as a steward. God sends His Spirit to you, and His Spirit cries out in you before you can cry out for yourself: "Abba Father."

There will be fathers on earth with greater and lesser skills, but all of them will fall short. Some of them may fall terribly short of the fatherhood of God. Nonetheless, I bless you with a magnificent work by the Spirit of sonship who teaches your own spirit how to trust the Father when you have been betrayed by earthly fathers. I bless you with knowing the security and the joy of the Father's relationship with you. I bless you with experiencing deep in your spirit the joy, the pleasure on the Father's face when you turn to Him, when you leave the commotion of the world and run to Him as a little child would. I bless you with deep healing that comes to your generational lines through experiencing, in a multitude of different ways, the lesson of the Spirit of sonship. I bless you with seeing the joy of the Father, the wisdom of the Father, the patience of the Father, the kindness of the Father, the creativity of the Father, and the humor of the Father.

Above all else, __________, the name of Abba Father is deeply rooted in security. Where your father may not have kept you safe, where other fathers may even have violated your boundaries, I bless you with full development in your life with a profound sense of safety. This can only come to those who intimately know the heart of their heavenly Father, not just His strength. As God calls you to minister the Father's heart to others throughout the various chapters of your life, I bless you with ministering from a full cup. I bless you with seeing the Father in a myriad of ways and having richly textured teachings about the Father which you will present to a needy world.

I bless you with knowing the Father in a way that erases the line between the sacred and the secular. I bless you with seeing Abba Father and having intimacy, safety, joy, and security with Him in the church, out of the church, at work, in your home, in times of pain and times of joy. I bless you with raising the standard in your community for an understanding of Abba Father. I bless the Spirit of sonship that He may do a perfect work in you, releasing the full fragrance of who you are, which can only come from those who have been perfectly fathered. I bless your essence as a person. I bless you with going back to your childhood and filling in the areas that were not properly fathered the first time around. I bless you with celebrating Abba Father by manifesting Him in who you are in your community, as a contagious example of someone who has tasted and drunk deeply of the work of the Spirit of sonship. I bless you, beloved child, in the Name of the Father and of the Son and the Holy Spirit. Amen.

Respond with your spirit...

Write your thoughts, etc.

Blessing Your Soul

Legacy[72]

Dear Soul,

In a world that can't see the value of investing in tomorrow, you are a treasure and a delight with your vision for the generations. May your tribe increase and multiply.

I bless you, soul, with having the tenacity to defend a narrow focus. your enemy of your soul will be [a] myriad [of] good things that will dilute the core things. May you not be distracted or diminished by the good in your relentless pursuit of the best.

Appendix 6

Scripture Selections for Crafting Blessings

Bible Passages for Words of Blessing
-Bill Gothard

Scriptures Suitable for Crafting a Blessing
-Terry and Melissa Bone

Scripture Selections for Crafting Blessings

Bible Passages for Words of Blessing[73]

A list of prayer-related passages in the New Testament that can easily be adapted as a blessing upon others.

Romans 15:5-6
Romans 15:13
1 Corinthians 1:4-9
1 Corinthians 16:23
2 Corinthians 1:2-7
2 Corinthians 2:14
2 Corinthians 13:7-9
Galatians 6:18
Ephesians 1:3-10
Ephesians 1:15-23
Ephesians 3:14-21
Ephesians 6:19-21
Ephesians 6:23-24
Philippians 1:3-6
Philippians 1:9-11
Philippians 4:6-8
Colossians 1:3-6
Colossians 1:9-14
Colossians 4:2-4
1 Thessalonians 1:2-3
1 Thessalonians 3:12-13
1 Thessalonians 5:23-24
1 Thessalonians 5:28
2 Thessalonians 1:11-12
2 Thessalonians 2:16-17
2 Thessalonians 3:5
2 Thessalonians 3:16
1 Timothy 1:12
2 Timothy 4:22
Philemon 1:4-7
Hebrews 13:20-21
1 Peter 1:3-9
1 Peter 5:10-11
2 Peter 1:2-4
2 Peter 3:18
2 John 1:3
3 John 1:2-3

Scriptures Suitable for Crafting a Blessing [74]

Some passages of the Scripture, such as Psalm 128, were actually written as blessings. Hundreds more are phrased in such a way as to be easily incorporated into a written or spoken blessing. Below is a small sample to get you started:

Blessings in Christ	Ephesians 1:3
Chosen by God	Ephesians 1:4, 11
Obedience and Long Life	Deuteronomy 5:33; 30:19-20
Rewards for Kindness	Ruth 2:12
For a Child to Prosper	1 Kings 2:1-3
Family Blessing	Psalm 128
The "Marriage Bed"	Proverbs 5:18-19
Fertility	Genesis 24:60; Deuteronomy 28:11
Prosperity in Business	Deuteronomy 15:10, Psalm 37:25-26, Proverbs 19:17, 22:9; Malachi 3:10-11
Tithing	Malachi 3:10-11
Physical Health	3 John 1
Peace and Holiness	1 Thessalonians 5:23
Wisdom and Revelation	Ephesians 1:17
Wisdom	Proverbs 3:12-18
Spiritual Insight	Ephesians 1:18-19
Spiritual Power	Ephesians 3:15-17
Blessings in Trials	Matthew 5:4, 10,11
Spiritual Hunger & Humility	Matthew 5:3, 5-9

Don't stop at these!
Now that you understand the idea, as you read the Bible, look for more Scriptures that are written in such a manner to be suitable to include in any kind of blessing.

Appendix 7

Author's Sample Blessings

Bible School Commencement
Chaplaincy Induction
Police Services
Jubilee Blessing (Fiftieth Milestone)
Name Blessing Keepsake

Author's Sample Blessings

Bible School Commencement

I had the honor of blessing my fellow graduates at the first Commencement Ceremony of Kingdom Bible Training Center in November 2015.

The meaning of the word "bless" in Greek is "to eulogize"—to speak well of someone. It is therefore fitting that we would begin by first blessing the Lord, our God and Father.

- *Bless the Lord, O my soul; And all that is within me, bless His holy Name! Bless the Lord, O my soul, and forget not all His benefits* (Psalm 103:1-2).
- *Blessing, and glory, and wisdom, and thanksgiving, and honour, and power, and might, be unto our God for ever and ever. Amen* (Rev 7:12).

Graduates, in the Name of the Lord, we bless the diligence, commitment, and concentration you have shown in doing your best for God. We bless you as workers who accurately handle the Word of truth. May the Word of God be profitable in you, making you complete and proficient, well-fitted and thoroughly equipped for every good work (2 Timothy 2:15, 3:16-17).

According to Isaiah 61:3, may the Lord bless you as an oak of righteousness; lofty, strong, and magnificent; distinguished for uprightness, justice and right standing with God, the planting of the Lord by which He shall be glorified.

By the power and authority of the Name of Jesus, I now pronounce over your life the very words God gave Aaron and the priests to bless the people and put His Name upon them.

The Lord bless you and keep you…

- The Lord bless you with His divine empowerment. The Lord bless you with His mantle and anointing to represent heaven here on earth in the destiny and realm of influence to which He has called you.
- The Lord keep you—guard, preserve, and protect you with His mighty hand, His Holy Spirit, His precious blood, His Word, His Name which is above every name, and with angelic interventions. May you be kept from every kind of evil.

The Lord make His face shine upon you and be gracious unto you…

- The Lord bless you with the radiance of His face. As God's face shines upon you, may you live under an open heaven with revelation, wisdom, understanding, creative ability and prosperity freely breaking forth. May you reflect the shimmer of God's glory, ever shining like stars of true Light in your generation and beyond.
- The Lord be gracious unto you, causing all grace—His supernatural, manifold grace—to abound in your life continuously, so that you will always have sufficiency in everything and an abundance in every good work.

The Lord lift up His countenance upon you and give you His peace.

- The Lord bless you with an ever-increasing consciousness of God's face turned favorably towards you. May you cherish His nearness and attentiveness as He guides you with His eyes.

- The Lord give you His peace—His Shalom. May you possess His wholeness and harmony in spirit, soul, and body, and in every area of life. According to Romans 16:20, may the God of Peace crush Satan under your feet.

With this blessing, the Name of the Lord, "I AM WHO I AM," shall remain upon you as a people belonging to God, a people set apart to make His marvelous glory and excellence known. Now and forever more; so shall it be, in the Name of Jesus. Amen.

Let us seal this blessing impartation in prayer:

Heavenly Father, we thank you for honoring us with your manifold blessing, not because of what we did or did not do, but because of all that Jesus has accomplished on our behalf. Lord Jesus, let your covenant blood now be a seal on these spoken blessings for all eternity. In the authority of your Name, we pray, Amen.

CHAPLAINCY INDUCTION[75]

Global Chaplaincy Center gave me the honor of imparting the blessing at the induction of its first thirty-nine chaplains in September 2017.

Inductees, I call your spirit to attention. Listen to the Word of the Lord and possess from the Father of Glory the impartation of what the Apostle Paul had prayed in Ephesians 1. These blessings were redeemed in Christ Jesus and the Apostle Paul petitioned the Father for you to experience them. Today, we bring them from the heavens to you by the power of the Holy Spirit.

We bless you with the spirit of wisdom and revelation [of insight into mysteries and secrets] in the [deep and intimate] knowledge of God. We bless you as a carrier of the presence and heart of God the Father, who is the Father of Compassion and the God of All Comfort. May you deeply experience the Father's compassion and comfort in your time of need so that you can, in turn, extend comfort, love and warmth to others in their time of need.

We bless you with an enlightened understanding. May the eyes of your heart be flooded with light, giving you a clear vision of this hope to which God has called you into chaplaincy. As one set apart for God, may you freely partake of the riches of His glorious inheritance with which He has blessed you. With this gift of supernatural understanding, you will know in every situation what, when, and how to minister God's grace and power to those in need.

We bless you even more with an enlightened understanding of the immeasurable, unlimited and surpassing greatness of God's power which is in you and for you as one who believes. May you be empowered with this same power which God demonstrated when He exerted His mighty strength in Christ, raised Him from the dead and seated Him at His [own] right hand in the heavenly [places]. May this power of God's might open doors for you according to His will for your life.

May you know, believe, and become increasingly settled in your seat of authority in Christ, knowing that you were raised with Christ and seated with Him—far above all rule and authority, all power and dominion, and every name that is named [above every title that can be conferred].

Today, we invoke God's blessing of provision from 2 Corinthians 9:8, for every dimension of your life and chaplaincy service: "And God is able to make all grace (every favor and earthly blessing) come to you in abundance, abound to you, so that you will always have sufficiency in everything, you may have an abundance for every good deed."

Now, receive in your spirit the impartation of your heavenly Father's mantle, anointing and authority to speak blessings for the transformation of lives wherever you may be called to serve. Receive the anointing oil of the Holy Spirit filling you. Receive this anointing to the point of overflowing so that it will gush out from your innermost being, cloth you with the glorified presence of God and infuse the words of your mouth with supernatural grace and power! Receive! In the Name of Jesus Christ of Nazareth.

"The Lord bless you and keep you; The Lord make His face shine upon you, And be gracious to you; The Lord lift up His countenance upon you, And give you peace."

The Name of the Lord is placed upon you, and you are blessed in the Name of the Father, the Son and the Holy Spirit. Amen.

Toronto Police Service

I was honored to represent the body of Christ in imparting this blessing to the Chief of Police and the Toronto Police Service at the Jesus in the City Pastor's Breakfast of March 30, 2017.

As a representative of the local churches, ministries and organizations in the city of Toronto, it is my privilege to impart the blessing of God on the Toronto Police Service.

Let's all release our faith together for this blessing impartation:

Heavenly Father, we bless you first of all as the Eternal One from whom all blessings flow. We bless you Lord Jesus, for giving us access to the Father's blessings.

Now, to the men and women of the Toronto Police Service:

On this ground of unity, one with each other, and as representatives of heaven's will on earth, we release God's commanded blessing of life over the entire police service, corporately and individually.

You are God's established authority. We bless you into a new season of exceptional honor in which your service will come into greater alignment with God's intent for this city and its people. This new season into which you are about to embark is also a season of increase. It is a season of increased WISDOM, STATURE, AND FAVOR according to the Word of God from Luke Chapter 2, Verse 52.

- May you receive WISDOM from God and an infusion of creative ideas and supernatural strategies to confront and resolve the challenges facing our city.
- May you surpass the STATURE you have attained so far, and in

time to come be highly regarded for your standards of integrity, justice, and compassion.

- Finally, may you abound in FAVOR with God and with those you serve. May God's favor surround you as a shield of protection and may the grace of God enable you to strengthen relationships with our diverse communities, especially the younger generation and youth at risk.

We seal this blessing in the Name of Jesus and declare that by His authority this blessing is established in the earth as it is in heaven.

God bless you, Toronto Police Service.

Jubilee Blessing (Fiftieth Milestone)

In proclaiming this Jubilee Blessing of God, we stand on the Word of Leviticus 25:10-14.

> 10 *And you shall consecrate the fiftieth year, and proclaim liberty throughout all the land to all its inhabitants. It shall be a Jubilee for you; and each of you shall return to his possession, and each of you shall return to his family.*
>
> 11 *That fiftieth year shall be a Jubilee to you; in it you shall neither sow nor reap what grows of its own accord, nor gather the grapes of your untended vine.*
>
> 12 *For it is the Jubilee; it shall be holy to you; you shall eat its produce from the field.*
>
> 13 *In this Year of Jubilee, each of you shall return to his possession.*
>
> 14 *And if you sell anything to your neighbor or buy from your neighbor's hand, you shall not oppress one another.*

We bless you _____________ *(fill in the name)*, as a New Covenant believer in Christ, to possess the fulfillment of your Jubilee Blessing. Let this Jubilee proclamation of Jesus from Luke chapter 4, settle deeply into your spirit.

> 18 *"The Spirit of the Lord is on me, because he has anointed me to proclaim good news to the poor. He has sent me to proclaim freedom for the prisoners and recovery of sight for the blind, to set the oppressed free,*
>
> 19 *to proclaim the year of the Lord's favor."*
>
> 21 *"Today this scripture is fulfilled in your hearing."*

Jesus Christ Himself proclaims "good news" over you: "Your Year of Jubilee is here!"

- Your heavenly Father watches over His Word, and by His authority, the manifestation of your Jubilee blessings shall come forth.

- May the Lord bless you with an abundance of grace to consecrate and set apart this Jubilee year unto Him so that every good intention of your heavenly Father's heart for you can be accomplished.

- The Lord bless your spirit, soul and body to experience this Jubilee Year as a year of **liberty** for yourself and others in your circle of influence; a year of **repossession and restoration**; a year of **reconciliation**; a year of **fruitfulness**; a year of **increase**; a year of **supernatural provision**; and a year of **safety and total well-being** in all areas of life.

- We plead the blood of Jesus over every ungodly experience in your past and proclaim your complete redemption in Christ. We bless you out of all past hurt, pain, loss and disappointment. By the grace of God, may you freely release all those who have wronged you in one way or another, so that you may freely possess the fullness of your Jubilee Blessing.

- We pronounce over you complete freedom from all forms of oppression (physical, spiritual, emotional, relational, and financial). You shall oppress no one, and no one shall oppress you, for you shall live in perpetual Jubilee by the grace of God and the power of the Holy Spirit.

- May the Holy Spirit enable you to experience a **lasting Jubilee** in your inner being as you mature into your spiritual identity of Sonship. Above all, we bless you to walk in the full liberty of the Spirit of the Son at work in your heart, granting you His freedom from every kind of bondage.

- By virtue of the proclamation of this Jubilee Year, we bless you into **new beginnings!**
- This is the acceptable year of the Lord to **repossess your possessions**! This is the year that the full favor of God abounds to you for **increase**!

In this Jubilee Year and beyond, we bless you in the name of the Father, the Son, and the Holy Spirit. Amen.

Name Blessing Keepsake

Colleen

Inherent Meaning

Maiden

Spiritual Significance

Excellent Virtue

On this momentous occasion of your 40th Birthday, we bless you with the unlocking of the hidden treasures in the meanings of your name.

In the natural, you are a happily married woman with children. Yet, in your spirit, you possess the timeless excellent virtue of a maiden. Like Mary of Nazareth, you are destined for the extraordinary and exceptional.

It is your God-given birthright to bring forth in your unique sphere of influence that which is "first-of-its-kind" to the glory and honor of your Abba Father.

We bless your spirit to be guided by the Holy Spirit in releasing its riches of wisdom, knowledge, and understanding to accomplish the glorious purpose you have been chosen to pioneer.

Wise people are builders— they build families, businesses, communities. And through intelligence and insight their enterprises are established and endure. Because of their skilled leadership the hearts of people are filled with the treasures of wisdom and the pleasures of spiritual wealth.
Proverbs 24:3–4 TPT

Great favor is upon you, for you have believed every word spoken to you from the Lord.

Luke 1:45 TPT

Rev. Marva Tyndale

TESTIMONIALS

A Father's Blessing

In 2010 my fiancé and I attended a birthday blessing for the son of a very close friend. This was my first exposure to the blessing. I did not know that what I was about to witness would radically transform my thinking about a father's blessing of his children.

Rev. Marva Tyndale was the special guest and she first spoke briefly about the blessing. As she did, I began to feel a void, an emptiness, from a deep place I did not fully understand. In blessing the child, she reached back to his conception, life in the womb, birth, and infancy. She blessed his present childhood stage and projected a blessing for the later stages of his life (teen years, adulthood, and finally, the senior years).

Her reference to the forefathers of the Bible and the significance of spoken blessings being passed down from a father to his sons and daughters impacted me. I recognized that at this point in my adult life, the void that was exposed needed immediate corrective action. This led me back to my dad who had also missed out on this blessing impartation.

By the time I got married, and later in 2013 when our son was on the way, I was equipped with "tools" to take the needed action as a husband and a father who blessed his family. I felt privileged to bless my wife and our coming together. During the pregnancy, Rev. Marva facilitated the "baby welcome blessing" for our son, and she blessed us as new parents. I am now the father of two boys with a heightened sense of the importance of blessing them.

The beauty in all of this is how the Lord opened the door for me to connect with my dad, at a deeper spiritual level by doing for him what hadn't been done for me. It was a joy to bless him in the company of my mom and some of his closest friends. The tears he shed that day were real because, like myself, there was a void in him from never having been blessed by his dad.

Rev. Marva Tyndale has championed a very important plan of action step to heal generational brokenness and gaps. The work to close that gap begins with me as a father and a husband. I am setting in motion a continuous pattern of blessing for generations to come. My sons will grow up knowing that they have been blessed by their dad and will, by God's grace, do the same for their children and grandchildren. Nothing is impossible when we speak the blessings God has designed for the human family.

—*Mark Green*

Thank you for such a powerful blessing on my birthday. Listening to the words God deposited in your heart for me validated my purpose and the call that I believe God has placed on my life. It was eye-opening to learn the meanings and significance of my name. My heart was blessed to hear such a commanding proclamation over my life. I am so very grateful that you took the time to hear from the Lord and spoke His words of blessing over me. May God continue to bless and keep you as you serve Him faithfully.

—*Colleen Miller-Blake*

In May 2010, Rev. Marva Tyndale introduced me to the power and importance of spoken blessings. It opened my spiritual eyes to new revelations and truths; using our words to impart life, to redeem and restore what's ours in Christ, and as a spring board into new seasons. It also revealed to me that our words can curse and delay God's original plans for our lives.

My family and I immediately started to develop the practice of speaking blessing over our lives, including the day of our birth, our gender, birth order, physical, mental and spiritual health. We also blessed our homes and encouraged others to do likewise. Our lives have not been the same since Rev. Marva introduced us to this powerful "tool" of blessing. We use it on a daily basis and on special occasions. Today, I am a blessing agent for my family, friends and youth, as I serve God. The blessing is a central part of my life.

Hebrews 4:12 resonates with me when I ponder the power of blessing: "For the word of God is alive and active. Sharper than any double-edged sword, it penetrates even to dividing soul and spirit, joints and marrow; it judges the thoughts and attitudes of the heart."

—*Michelle Edwards*

It all came about on my 26th birthday. I had shared with a friend that I desired to have a blessing ceremony. That day, in the presence of my family and friends, Marva pronounced over me the meanings of my name, my life message and my life Scriptures.

Name meanings: Boundary Line and Protected.

My life message: One who is secure in the Lord's protection and provision.

My life Scriptures: Psalm 16:5-6 and Isaiah 60:17b-18.

That day, it was as if the gates of heaven opened up over me and the Lord spoke directly into my innermost being. My life Scriptures launched me on a brand new, less destructive trajectory. My story, imperfect as it was, now became marked by God's redemptive love that restored and established my life with healthy walls and boundaries.

The longing questions in my heart about acceptance, safety and provision, destiny and purpose were once and for all answered. I take it as no coincidence that I have since had such clarity in what I am called to do (my purpose) and who will share this journey with me—my best friend and husband of eight adventurous years, M. Anthony Giscômbe. It is no surprise that our children (4-year-old boy and 2-year-old girl) have received the blessing before birth through Marva's ministry. Declaring and pronouncing the meaning of their names over them is something my husband and I practice regularly.

—*Sabrina Giscômbe*

The "Weight" of the Blessing

While visiting Trinidad in March 2018, I had a dream that gave me a fresh revelation of the weight and power of God that words of blessing convey. The dream followed a night of interceding for my community there. My intercession had centered around appropriating Warren Marcus' amplified interpretation of the Aaronic blessing, and it was intermingled with a flow of prayer that came from each sentence of the blessing.

In the dream, I was in Mississauga, Canada with others from the Peel House of Prayer intercessory team. We were engaged in some sort of crisis intervention involving parents, their children and schools in the Mavis/Eglinton area. It stood out to me that this intercession was for families. We were asking the Lord for direction because we sensed that we were carrying an anointing as "solutionists" to influence what was happening in this community. Our impact was negligible at first, then the Holy Spirit's wisdom kicked in and I knew that the key was not prayer, but blessing.

I began to release over the families what I called "supernaturally graced words of blessing," and was keenly aware that the words I spoke were not 'my' words. Heaven was intervening in the words of blessing I released. Each word carried an apostolic weight (authority) that commanded the atmosphere to shift and unlocked heaven in the hearts of those who heard the words, despite their stormy circumstances. Earth responded to heaven's touch. Families acknowledged and glorified God, and a door was opened for evangelism and prayer.

When I woke up in the morning, my whole being was alight and alive from this glorious experience of the blessing. Completely in awe of God, this confession flowed out to Him: "Lord, I never knew there was such weight and power in blessing." I was contemplating the remarkable results that blessing had accomplished in comparison to the lesser impact that prayer had in this specific situation. I then understood the power of blessing as a significant key to unlock lives, communities and regions for prayer and evangelism to have the impact that heaven desires.

—*Rhonda McLeod*

In our culture, the concept of "blessings" has become a by-product of erroneous religious consumerism and has been frequently mistaken as a means to materialistic profit. As a result of this trend, the essence of the spoken blessing, as imparted by Rev. Marva Tyndale, becomes very significant and essential.

As I received the blessings imparted by Rev. Marva in a "Blessing Recovery Clinic," I recall being supernaturally transported to an unfinished place of my past. The blessings she spoke that day exposed hidden and elusive places in me that I had subconsciously overlooked or left unaddressed.

By the power of those words of blessing, the incomplete in me became complete. My "unfilled gaps" began to fill-up with truth. The promises of an unchanging God challenged my outlook on my spiritual birthrights! I knew in that moment that there was no longer any part of my life that had to be left unfinished or unreachable.

I understood that access to the blessings of my heavenly Father was available to me and to all who would believe and receive. The spoken blessing is now established as part of my life and in my family. I discovered its power to reconcile our past and transform our future, including that of generations to come! Rev. Marva is God's servant, called at this time to stand in the gap for us to ACCESS, ACTIVATE and IMPART the transformational truth found in the power of generational blessings!

—Jackie Nugent

We came out of a Hindu background in 2009, after receiving new life in Jesus Christ. We found out about the blessing through a dream I had in 2013, a few months before the birth of our first child, Benjamin. In this dream, I heard these words, "Pronounce a blessing before the flood gates are open." I knew nothing about spoken blessings until my spiritual Mom explained the dream to me. She said I needed to have the baby blessed in the womb and she knew exactly the person to do the blessing—Rev. Marva.

We had friends and family from the Christian and Hindu faith at the blessing ceremony. The impact was astonishing. We were all hearing about the seven life stages for the first time, and the blessings we had missed from the time of conception. It gave us great joy to know that even before being born, our baby was receiving in his spirit and heart words that welcomed him and put the favor of God on his identity and destiny. We learned a lot about the blessing and continued to speak blessing over our son from that day onward. Our second son, Nathaniel, was born in 2016, and he also started to receive the blessing in the womb.

The blessing is part of our life and we have had the opportunity to also speak blessings to others. We are grateful for the revelation given to Rev. Marva through our Lord Jesus Christ, concerning the power of the spoken words of blessings (Proverbs 18:21).

We thank God for His amazing power and work in our lives, also for His goodness and blessings over us. Pronouncing blessings over our lives releases God's power to bring us through even the toughest of times, gives us hope and strengthens us for His purpose. Faith arises when we speak what God has written, because the Word of God will always achieve the will of Heaven!

—*Dave & Hema Paul*

I was introduced to the concept of verbal blessings by Rev. Marva Tyndale in 2015. Initially, it was through a blessing she spoke over me at the end of a business meeting, followed by observing this pattern in her regular speech as she interacted with those around her. I was intrigued and wanted to learn more. After attending a conference hosted at her church and buying all the materials she recommended, I began to search out ways that I too could implement the verbal blessing in special events that I was part of.

My first opportunity came when I hosted the 70th birthday party of my spiritual mother. Rev. Marva helped me to craft a blessing appropriate for her age and stage in life. My spiritual mother was deeply touched that we had incorporated a blessing ceremony as part of the festivities.

Next, I started making plans for the gift of the verbal blessings that I had missed to be formally released over my life. I spoke with my senior pastor and we organized a beautiful, intimate event whereby my spiritual mentors and close friends gathered to speak the blessings for the seven major life stages over my life. They declared fruitfulness to be restored in all areas of my life.

The third major event where we used the verbal blessing was during the Induction Ceremony of thirty-nine new chaplains with the Global Chaplaincy Center. We wanted to impart the mantle for these chaplains to also be Blessing Ambassador. To this day, many of them still speak of the impact of the words spoken to them and what it ignited in their spirits. Truly, the gift of our words in speaking blessings changes the spiritual and natural atmosphere in which we live, breathe and operate.

Rev. Marva's newest book is a must in the collection of all pastors and leaders whose deepest desire is to serve people and see them walking in spiritual wholeness. Now, more than ever before, we need to share the verbal blessing and give people the life-changing gift of our words!

—*Korrie Silver*

Words cannot express how the power of the blessing has transformed my life. From the first time I was introduced to the blessing, I was intrigued to find out more.

I grew up with different kinds of abuse and my life was on a fast track for destruction. God used Rev. Marva Tyndale, through the leading of the Holy Spirit, to go back to the time of my conception and decree blessings into each border crossing of my life. The experience destroyed curses and freed me from my painful past.

What the devil tried to steal from me, God gave back to me; beyond anything I can imagine. I now walk in the power of Christ and in the authority the Lord has given to me.

The power of spoken blessings will change your life forever!

—*Pamela Smith*